The West Virginia Pepperoni Roll

The
WEST VIRGINIA PEPPERONI ROLL

Candace Nelson
with a foreword by Emily Hilliard

West Virginia University Press • 2017

First edition published 2017

Printed in Canada

ISBN:

Paper   978-1-943665-74-7

Library of Congress Cataloging-in-Publication Data
is available from the Library of Congress

Book and cover design by Than Saffel.
Cover images and all uncredited images are courtesy of the author or licensed by
West Virginia University Press.

MEMORIES ← *John Angotti*

"Whenever my mom would make pizza dough or loaves of bread and rolls, she'd save some leftover and stick pepperoni inside and make little ones. My God, they were like crack cocaine. My buddies, they'd flock like bees to honey. As a kid, growing up in an Italian household, we didn't go out to eat unless someone was getting married or dying. My mom cooked. My dad always said, his mother who came from Italy, they always talked about making these rolls with whatever was left over, a little salami, and they'd roll it up and bake it in the oven. . . . Most of the Italian Americans in North Central West Virginia came from San Giovanni in Fiore—my family included. We started this medical exchange program, a cultural exchange where two students from the medical school get chosen to go to the south of Italy, stay for a month and study the Italian medical system. They'll send doctors over here to study at the hospital under their specialty. . . . My family is from the town, and my dad always spoke highly of it, so there was this connection to my Italian heritage. It became the perfect fit for me. It actually changed my life and opened my mind to my heritage. . . . When my grandparents came to America, my grandmother said 'you're American now, you speak English, you assimilate into the culture.' But the next generation, we want to show we're proud and Italian—the family, the religion, the food. And pepperoni rolls are part of that."

—John Angotti, a Morgantown, WV, native and president of
Audia Caring Heritage Association in West Virginia

*We want to show we're proud and Italian—
the family, the religion, the food. And
pepperoni rolls are part of that.*

CONTENTS

Foreword ix

Author's Note xiii

Introduction 1

Origins 5

Bakeries from the Beginning 7

    Country Club Bakery 7

    Tomaro's Bakery 12

    D'Annunzio's Italian Bread (The Health Bread Company) 18

    Abruzzino's Italian Bakery 24

    Chico Bakery—Home of Julia's Pepperoni Rolls 28

    Colasessano's World Famous Pizza & Pepperoni Buns 34

    Rogers and Mazza's Italian Bakery (Marty's Bakery) 41

    Home Industry Bakery (A&M Bakery) 46

    The Donut Shop 52

    JR's Donut Castle 55

The Science of Making a Pepperoni Roll 59

    The Bread 59

    The Pepperoni 63

    Sticks vs. Slices (vs. Ground) 67

Pepperoni Roll Prevalence 73

School Lunches 73

Fundraisers 75

Gas Stations 76

Military 76

Ballparks, Arenas, and Stadiums 78

The Pepperoni Roll Makes Media Headlines 82

Pepperoni Roll Crusades 85

2013 CQ Roll Call Taste of America 85

You Can't Outsource the Pepperoni Roll 86

Pepperoni Roll Events 90

Golden Horseshoe Great Pepperoni Roll Cook-Off 90

West Virginia Three Rivers Festival 91

Other Fairs and Festivals 98

So Good It Should Be Illegal 105

Bakery Classifications 105

Legality in Other States 106

Official State Food 107

Pepperoni Rolls around the State: Where to Find Them 110

Keeping with Tradition 110

The Modern Pepperoni Roll 117

Adaptations for Dietary Concerns 124

The Great Pepperoni Roll Expansion: Recipes 126

Watson Coal Mine Pepperoni Rolls 127

Whitney Hatcher's Easy Pepperoni Rolls 129

Kaitlynn Anderson's Low-Carb and Gluten-Free Pepperoni Rolls 130

Momma's Hot Rolls 132

The Final Pepperoni 134

References 140

FOREWORD

By Emily Hilliard

In 2005, I began writing about "Nothing in the House" pies on a blog my friend Margaret and I started. The concept came from the book *The Study of American Folklore* by Jan Harold Brunvand and describes historical "Desperation pies"—vinegar pie and cracker pie and green tomato pie—that were made with few, cheap ingredients, and emerged out of times and places of economic hardship. These recipes are tied to rural areas, labor, and are part of regional food heritage, adapting and changing to suit and serve modern tastes, preferences, and contexts, as all traditions do.

In February of 2011, I had my first pepperoni roll, bought from the Donut Shop in Buckhannon on a trip through West Virginia. I didn't know it then, but my experiences in West Virginia since, paired with Candace's writing on the Mountain State's beloved handheld food, have revealed that pepperoni rolls firmly fit in the "Nothing in the House" food category. Similar to those Depression-era pies, pepperoni rolls were conceived of to use affordable and readily available ingredients and to fulfill the need for a quick and filling meal that a laborer—in this case, a coal miner—could eat on the job. Transcending their essential qualities as cheap, handy, and delicious snacks, pepperoni rolls are also a potent symbol of the state's labor history, immigrant contributions, and ever-evolving cultural heritage.

Emily Hilliard is the West Virginia state folklorist. Her food writing has been featured by NPR, the Southern Foodways Alliance, *Lucky Peach*, and the *Oxford Companion to Sugar and Sweets*, among others.

She writes the pie blog *Nothing in the House* at www.nothinginthehouse.com.

Fairmont baker and former miner Giuseppe "Joseph" Argiro, originally from Calabria, Italy, is credited with creating the first pepperoni roll in 1927. He had observed his fellow miners eating pepperoni with bread while at work, and decided to combine the two into an easily portable pocket food (miners have a history of inspiring delicious pocket foods—if you've ever had a Michigan pasty, you know what I'm talking about). Argiro founded the Country Club Bakery where he sold the rolls, and eventually passed the business on to his son Frank "Cheech" Argiro. It's still in operation today.

While the classic pepperoni roll uses pepperoni slices or sticks rolled in white bread dough, and does not include cheese, West Virginians have continued to adapt the recipe. Subsequent variations employ shredded pepperoni, cheese, and peppers, top the roll with chili or hot dog "sauce," use vegetarian "pepperoni," and even incorporate foods from other ethnic traditions like Jewish challah bread, Mexican queso blanco, and German pretzel dough. Recently, I learned of a sausage maker of Spanish heritage in Harrison County who makes a version with his homemade chorizo rather than pepperoni.

In *The West Virginia Pepperoni Roll,* Candace Nelson offers us an insider's take on the pepperoni roll, exploring the history, science, great pepperoni roll debates (sticks vs. slices, Sheetz vs. the people of West Virginia), cultural context, regional variations, and adaptations as only a native could. As the nature of my work as state folklorist takes me all over West Virginia, hungry both in appetite and in my quest to sample local traditional culture—including foods—I am grateful to have such a guide.

If you're not near West Virginia, there are, as Candace points out, many bakeries that ship their rolls. But the only way to get that fresh-from-the-oven taste pepperoni roll lovers crave is to make them yourself. Here's a recipe I've developed, adapted from Kendra Bailey Morris. I controversially favor slices over sticks, but you can alter it to your preferences. Otherwise, I stick to the classic—in my opinion, a good pepperoni roll needs no extra flavor or moisture, as the oil of the pepperoni roll is absorbed by the bread, creating that telltale orange hue along the edges.

Homemade Pepperoni Rolls

ADAPTED FROM KENDRA BAILEY MORRIS

Makes about 20 rolls, depending on size

INGREDIENTS

For the rolls:

- 1 package (2 1/4 teaspoons) active dry yeast
- ½ cup warm water
- ½ cup plus ½ teaspoon sugar
- 1–2 white potatoes, peeled and cut into large pieces
- ½ cup unsalted butter, very soft
- 1 teaspoon salt
- 1 egg
- 7–8 cups all-purpose flour
- 1–½ (about 1 pound) pepperoni stick, cut into thin slices

For the glaze:

- 1 tablespoon unsalted butter
- 2 teaspoons sugar
- 1 large egg

Homemade Pepperoni Rolls
continued

DIRECTIONS

1. In a small bowl, combine yeast, warm water, and ½ teaspoon sugar until yeast dissolves. Let stand at room temperature for 45 minutes until foamy.
2. Meanwhile, place potatoes in a pot with at least three cups of water (enough to make approximately 2 ½ cups leftover potato water) and cook until tender.
3. Pulse cooked potatoes and 2 ½ cups potato water in a blender. Add the ½ cup sugar, butter, and salt, blending well. Add the egg and blend 5 seconds more. Let mixture cool to lukewarm.
4. Once cool, pour potato mixture into the bowl of a stand mixer fitting with the paddle attachment, mixing in the yeast. Slowly add 4 cups of flour and beat until smooth. Add 3-4 more cups of flour and knead until the dough is fairly stiff but still a little sticky. Place dough in a large greased bowl and cover with plastic wrap. Place in the refrigerator for at least 8 hours or overnight. (Note: the dough will keep in the fridge for 5 to 6 days. Be sure to push down the dough at least once per day.)
5. When you're ready to bake, preheat the oven to 400 degrees F. Turn dough onto a floured board and cut into quarters. Continue to cut into roughly 20 small pieces. Take a piece of the dough and push it flat into a rectangle. Place 2-3 slices of pepperoni in the middle (overlapping and not stacking) and roll, pinching the ends of the dough to hold the pepperoni inside. Place on an ungreased baking sheet. Repeat until you've used up all of your dough and pepperoni.
6. In a small saucepan, melt the butter and sugar. Remove from the heat and let cool slightly. Add your egg and mix well. Brush tops of the rolls with this mixture, then bake them until golden brown, about 12 to 15 minutes. Enjoy!

AUTHOR'S NOTE

Pepperoni rolls were just like any other concession-stand food growing up. They were stocked alongside hot dogs and ice cream at the local swimming-pool snack shop, the softball-field concession stand, and any number of booths found at the local fairs and festivals. The best ones though? Easy—they came from fundraisers at my high school in Brooke County, WV (Go Brooke Bruins!).

What I didn't know growing up is that pepperoni rolls are specific to West Virginia, with deep roots in our state's coal-mining history. When I left my hometown of Wellsburg in the Northern Panhandle for West Virginia University, I met people from all over the country—many of whom had never heard of the piece of culinary gold that we call the pepperoni roll. How could this be? My first question was: "What did you sell in high school for fundraisers?"

Pepperoni rolls are mostly only found in West Virginia? Really? Wow. We have a secret snack! One so delicious that, growing up, my friends and I would trade the one or two crumpled dollars in our pockets for the doughy treat at school events. One so substantial that it composed the main portion of my lunches during my undergraduate studies at West Virginia University. One so ingrained in the West Virginia culinary lifestyle that as I entered my journalistic career I heard time and time again—as offshoots to the real stories I was covering—how much people enjoy them and take pride in offering them to those from outside of West Virginia.

When the pepperoni roll had the chance to become the official state food via a resolution during the legislative session in 2013, my editor at the then *Charleston Daily Mail*, Brad McElhinny, sent me to cover the story. I imagine I rolled my eyes at the seeming silliness of the assignment before panic set in: I had to go to the capitol for one of my first stories. Through a series of events, I can thank Brad for setting this book into motion. I can thank him for knowing what captures an audience and trusting me to do so. I can thank him for igniting a curiosity about how our state connects to food and a desire to learn about the people who will fight to no end to uphold the pepperoni roll's rightful spot among regional and national food contests and challenges. I can thank him for assigning me a multitude of pepperoni roll stories that garnered attention (both good and bad) and that led to unearthing this beautiful history, helping to tell a piece of West Virginia's story. Thanks, Brad.

"'Why don't you just eat pizza?' they said. 'Isn't it basically the same thing?' they said. It is <u>not</u> the same thing."

—Isabelle Shepherd, a Fort Ashby, WV, native
who moved to North Carolina and was dismayed by the lack of pepperoni rolls

INTRODUCTION

It's not a pizza pocket. Not a pizza turnover. No, not pepperoni bread. It's not a calzone or stromboli either. West Virginia is home to the **pepperoni roll**.

```
pep-per-o-ni roll \pe-pə-'rō-nē 'rōl\ n : a soft, golden
oval of slightly sweetened dough enveloping pepperoni that
leaches out spices and oils, flavoring the bread and creating a
reddish-orange color on the inside of the roll. Cheese and/or
sauce are optional. Originated and found almost exclusively
in West Virginia, a pepperoni roll can be a snack or meal.
```

In West Virginia, the pepperoni roll is ubiquitous—from convenience stores and fundraisers to bakeries and lunches—but it is seldom seen outside of state borders. Originally made as a utilitarian food for West Virginian coal miners, pepperoni rolls are now as connected to West Virginia as chili is to Cincinnati, as barbecue is to the Carolinas, as pizza is to New York. In fact, this humble recipe has gained cult status in the state—with native West Virginians gifting them to expatriates who miss the fluffy comfort food reminiscent of home. Some local bakeries will even ship to those out of the area who are craving a West Virginia pepperoni roll. "They're the state's greatest export since Jerry West!" said West Virginia expatriate Michael

Tomasky, *Newsweek/Daily Beast* special correspondent, who has introduced the culinary specialty to his friends.

Others from all around the state describe pepperoni rolls as downright divine. Chris Lewallen an Alderson native, said, "If Jesus were a West Virginian, he would have eaten a pepperoni roll at the Last Supper." Brendan Sherlock, a Morgantown native said, "Pepperoni rolls are God's perfect snack food. They're always a reliable, delicious meal you can get pretty much anywhere you look in West Virginia." Isabelle Shepherd, a Fort Ashby native who moved to North Carolina was dismayed by the lack of pepperoni rolls: "When I complained, I was met with misunderstanding. 'Why don't you just eat pizza?' they said. 'Isn't it basically the same thing?' they said. It is not the same thing. Also, they don't taste the same if they're not made in West Virginia, I'm positive."

In a state where regional treats abound—the wild leeks known as ramps; pawpaw fruits; coleslaw-topped hot dogs, crunchy-crusted but cold cheese-topped DiCarlo's Pizza; buckwheat pancakes; and decadent, calorie-loaded Tudor's biscuits for a sustaining breakfast—arguably, the food that has most defined West Virginia cuisine is the pepperoni roll. It keeps the culinary heart of West Virginia beating.

Opposite: Integrated shift of miners with tools and lunch buckets, Price Hill Colliery Company. Photographer unknown. Image courtesy of West Virginia and Regional History Collection, West Virginia University Libraries.

MEMORIES  *Tim Urbanic*

"I really didn't know of pepperoni rolls until I came to West Virginia [from Pennsylvania], which was a long time ago.... My family, unknowingly, was making these in a sense. My father was a coal miner. My mother made a pepperoni sandwich with egg to hold the sandwich together. She would sauté egg in the skillet. In the fifties, I was only six. She would put an egg to hold pepperoni together and put it between two pieces of bread, wrap it up in paper, and put it in my dad's lunch pail when he went into the mines. It kinda fits in what they were doing in West Virginia—making it something you could eat hot and cold. It was a great 'easy to eat' with one hand sandwich to eat down in the mine. The mine was always 54 degrees. So this was very filling and fulfilling taste-wise.... I think it's a really cool sandwich. I still grab one when I'm on the road sometimes.... I make them once in a while for family and staff at the restaurant. Not in competition with people who have special recipes down pat and how its always been made—I feel strongly about what an important contribution all the coal miners made to this country and I like everything about the history of coal mining. While it is slowly going by the wayside, I see a bright future for other alternatives now."

—Tim Urbanic, co-owner and chef at Cafe Cimino in Sutton, WV

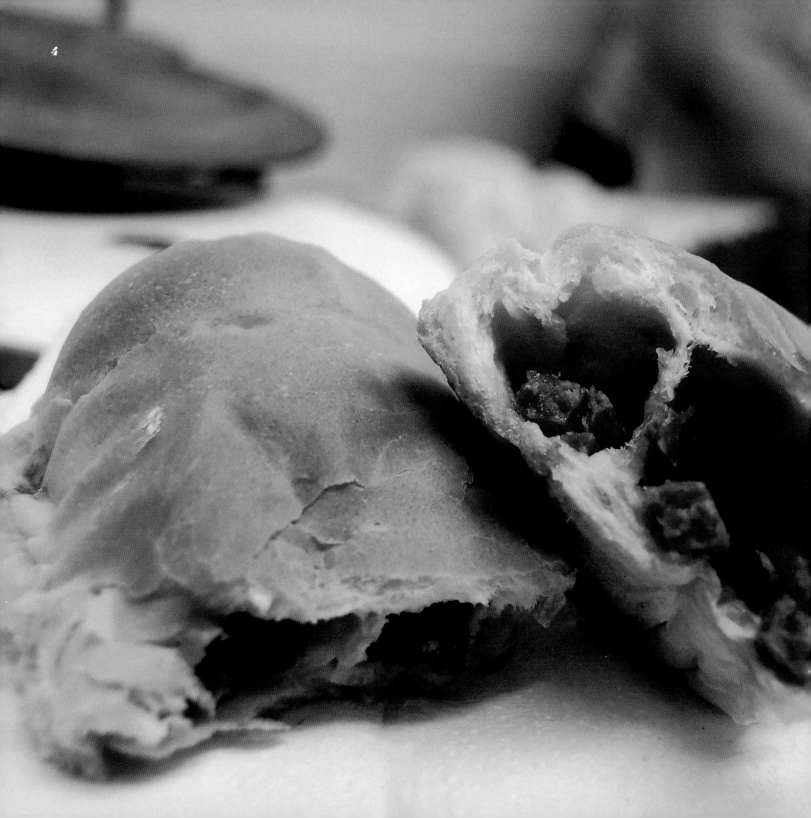

ORIGINS

Coal has played a large role in the economy and culture of West Virginia, and the pepperoni roll attributes its roots to coal—coal miners in particular. Hungry ones. The origin of the pepperoni roll is most commonly traced back to North Central West Virginia, specifically the town of Fairmont, and around the year 1927. Fairmont has since dubbed itself the "pepperoni roll capitol of the world."

In the early twentieth century, Italians flocked to West Virginia because of the booming coal and railroad industry. Giuseppe "Joseph" Argiro, who had emigrated from Calabria, Italy, in 1920 to work in a Clarksburg-area coal mine, left the coal industry and started a new venture: the People's Bakery on Robinson Street in downtown Fairmont. The former miner had noticed fellow Italians bringing a piece of bread and a stick of pepperoni to lunch in the mines. The no-frills lunch was portable, inexpensive, nonperishable, and tasty. Sometime between 1927 and 1938, Argiro decided to combine the spicy pepperoni and fluffy roll into one for commercial use. It is likely the first creators of the pepperoni roll were home cooks—wives, in particular, of coal miners looking to fill coal miners' bellies.

Argiro experimented with his new snack, developing bread-dough recipes,

Sometime between 1927 and 1938, Giuseppe Argiro decided to combine sticks of spicy pepperoni and a fluffy roll into one item: the pepperoni roll.

testing pepperonis, and changing up the proportions, until he was pleased with the final product. The compact, convenient roll could be eaten with one hand and required no heat, refrigeration, or utensils. The pepperoni roll became a hit and eventually sold by the dozen at the bakery.

Argiro is most often credited with creating the first pepperoni roll, and he marketed and produced it for a large consumer base. In the 1940s, when the bakery moved to a red brick building with white awnings, which sits just back off Country Club Road, the pepperoni rolls cost around forty-five cents per dozen—less than four cents per roll. The Country Club location would come to churn out hundreds per day, five days per week, and provide the namesake now synonymous with the creation of the pepperoni roll.

Zach Peters   MEMORIES

"Coal miners have to be at work early, usually underground by 6 a.m., and some guys drive near an hour so [pepperoni rolls are] something that a lot of guys got to eat. I would always get them at the Little General Exxon in Van, WV, on my way to Wharton when I worked at the Campbell's Creek No. 10 mine. I usually ate a pepperoni roll, a package of Grandma's cookies, and a milk for breakfast. Basically, people got them because the gas station closest to work always had them and [they are] easy to eat while driving and operating equipment. And, it takes one hand and doesn't fall apart when you eat it."

—Zach Peters, Madison, WV, native and former coal miner

BAKERIES FROM THE BEGINNING

1211 COUNTRY CLUB RD.
FAIRMONT, WV 26554
304-363-5690

Country Club Bakery

Giuseppe Argiro, most commonly credited with being the originator of the commercialized pepperoni-roll staple, passed on his popularized recipe on to his son, Frank "Cheech" Argiro, who took over Country Club Bakery in 1963 following his father's death. Cheech went on to run the bakery for more than thirty years, until 1997 when Chris Pallotta, who was a family friend of the Argiros, purchased the business.

Pallotta grew up about a mile from the bakery, eating pepperoni rolls about three times a week as a kid—he knows what they should taste like. So Pallotta stays true to the original 1927-era recipe, steering clear of any chemical preservatives. "We keep it real simple," Pallotta said. "We use basic bread ingredients, high-quality pepperoni and keep everything very fresh." His bakery cooks pepperoni rolls five days a week (closed on Wednesdays and Sundays), making three hundred to four hundred dozen a day—or as many as

Above: Country Club Bakery, located at 1211 Country Club Road, Fairmont, WV 26554, is most often credited as the first shop to commercially sell the pepperoni roll.

Far left: Country Club Bakery received the West Virginia Three Rivers Festival Professional Pepperoni Roll Bake-Off Champion Award.

Left: A dozen pepperoni rolls sold for about forty-five cents in the 1940s. Country Club Bakery, in 2016, sold a dozen pepperoni rolls for $14.99, which equals out to about $1.25 per pepperoni roll.

forty-eight hundred individual rolls. "Other bakeries may do them every other day or two times a week," he said, "but people are looking for a fresh product, a reasonably priced product, and a good product."

Good things take time, which is why Pallotta and his ten-person team arrive at the bakery at about 2:30 in the morning to mix all the dough. One woman has been at the bakery longer than Pallotta, and one man has been delivering the pepperoni rolls for a decade. Even Pallotta's own grandmother worked for quite some time. "She's eighty-two now," Pallotta said, "but she would come in and more or less hang out with the customers, and everyone enjoyed seeing her."

After mixing the dough, the team lets it rise in a wooden bin, which imparts some flavor. Then, they cut the dough into weights. Country Club weighs out about 2.5-ounce buns and rolls them with three five- to six-inch strips of pepperoni—two on one side, one on the other. Those sticks? They're cut from three-pound blocks. In one month, the bakery uses about two tons of pepperoni. Next, it's off to bake, cool, and package. Individuals and restaurants often use their own sauces and cheese to make the pepperoni rolls into a meal.

When most customers walk into the restaurant, Pallotta said, the first thing from their mouths is, "Oh, I just love the smell of fresh bread." But after seventeen years, he doesn't smell it anymore. "All my clothes smell like bread," he said, "but I wouldn't have it any other way."

Far left: Giuseppe Argiro removes a loaf of bread from the oven during the late 1950s. Image Credit: Larry Argiro, *Goldenseal* 32, no. 1.

Left: Frank "Cheech" Argiro took over Country Club Bakery in 1963 following his father's death. Image Credit: *Goldenseal* 32, no. 1.

Far left: Frank "Cheech" Argiro, center, works to assemble pepperoni rolls with his crew. Image Credit: *Goldenseal* 32, no. 1.

Left: Misty Whiteman has worked at Country Club Bakery for about thirty-five years and runs the ovens.

Far left: Country Club Bakery employees cut sticks of pepperoni by hand and roll three five- to six-inch sticks in each roll.

Left: Country Club Bakery cuts fresh dough into about 2.5-ounce buns.

Top left: Chris Pallotta, center, is the current owner of Country Club Bakery. The ten-person Country Club Bakery team arrives early in the morning to begin baking.

Lower left: Country Club Bakery workers form an assembly line for the pepperoni roll process—from cutting and weighing dough balls to adding the spicy stick pepperoni and prepping for baking. Country Club Bakery produces about three hundred to four hundred dozen pepperoni rolls per day.

April through December is the busiest time of the year, especially during the summer when people are stopping through on road trips. Pallotta said it's part of a ritual for Fairmont natives or expatriates when in town: they get a dozen pepperoni rolls from Country Club Bakery, then head to Yann's Hot Dog Stand for a dozen hot dogs, then hit up Colasessano's for a pizza—the Fairmont trifecta.

"We've been on the Food Network and other shows, and there are always little stories in the media, so we get people who say 'we heard of your bakery and pinned it on our map and were driving through and wanted to stop to see what it's all about,'" he said. "People will grab them as they head out to the beach or go to a ball game. The reason they were invented still rings true today: they're convenient."

But people who can't make it to Fairmont aren't out of luck: Pallotta ships his rolls anywhere in the continental United States in about two days. "I ship them all over the country, mostly to people who have lived here or who had family who lived here," he said. Sometimes his customers will send the rolls to military bases, but since it can take up to a week to ship internationally, Pallotta doesn't do this himself—he never wants the quality of the product to be in question.

Pallotta knows that as the producer of a regional delicacy, he has competition—there are around a dozen other bakeries in the surrounding counties alone with "hundreds of variations." But this doesn't worry Pallotta: "We're the original."

MEMORIES *Roxy Todd*

"I've heard some people from Kanawha and Wyoming Counties swear that the lunch ladies at their school cafeterias made the best homemade pepperoni rolls. I've never tried those, but I bet they're delicious.

"The first time I tasted a pepperoni roll, I wasn't even living in West Virginia—we were in Montana. One of my roommates, Jeremy, was from Buckhannon, and his mom makes the most amazing pepperoni rolls in the universe, so she sent him some in a care package. He made all of us pepperoni rolls for breakfast one morning. That experience, honestly, may have been one thing that made me think, I want to move to West Virginia.

"My husband Joey is originally from Fairmont, so the first pepperoni rolls I ever had in West Virginia were from the Country Club Bakery. I'll have to be honest, I'm torn between Country Club and Tomaro's as the best pepperoni rolls you can buy. One time we took a bag of Tomaro's pepperoni rolls on a road trip. We got to the bakery around nine in the morning, when they were just pulling the rolls out of the oven. If you really want the authentic pepperoni roll experience, you have to get to these bakeries that have been making them for decades. And you have to get there early. If you've only had gas-station pepperoni rolls, you haven't had the real thing.

"That's why the Sheetz controversy was a little bit silly to me. I mean I get it; they were trying to sell West Virginians Pennsylvania-made pepperoni rolls. That's nearly as insulting as when people forget that Virginia and West Virginia are two different states. You can't outsource the heritage food from out of state. That's just the most absurd thing imaginable, and I'm glad people from West Virginia stuck to their values. When I spoke to a spokesperson from Sheetz, they seemed totally caught off guard by the whole thing. They had no idea what they were doing when they tried to switch suppliers. I'm not entirely happy with how it turned out. . . . To get the West Virginia–made rolls, you have to go in search of them. But I get it, gas stations want food that has a lot of preservatives and can sit on a shelf for months. That's not what pepperoni rolls are meant to be. But sadly, that's what a lot of people think pepperoni rolls are.

"But seriously folks, no gas-station pepperoni roll is the real true deal. I've eaten them, and I've enjoyed them, but there's just no comparison to what Tomaro's or Country Club bakes. And everyone needs to go there, talk to the people who've been making them for thirty years to really appreciate what this food is and the story behind the food. It's so much more than white bread with a pepperoni baked inside. It's the people who make it what it is.

"Oh, and sticks, not circles—obviously. Although, the pepperoni rolls Jane Martin made and sent in a care package to my roommate, Jeremy, were made with these big pepperoni circles. So maybe, if you're making homemade, the rules are a little different. Oh and in the springtime, Jane also makes ramparoni rolls, with fresh ramps baked into the bread along with the pepperoni. I mean, that should be the recruitment strategy for bringing in new people to West Virginia.

"That's partly what motivated me to move here."

—Roxy Todd, producer of *Inside Appalachia* and creator of *Travelling 219*, an oral history project that was awarded a national award of merit from the American Association for State and Local History

BAKERIES

411 N. FOURTH STREET
CLARKSBURG, WV 26301
304-622-0691
TOMAROSBAKERY.COM

Tomaro's Bakery

But the birthplace of the pepperoni roll is not uncontested: Tomaro's Bakery, located in Clarksburg, WV, claims the beginning of the savory staple just as likely could have been a few miles south of Fairmont, right in the Glen Elk district of their city.

"Everybody goes back and forth on who made the first pepperoni roll," said Marisa Brunett, who co-owns Tomaro's Bakery with her brother John and mother Janice. "It was either Country Club Bakery or us. They started pretty close to the same time." Brunett said her grandfather was friends with the Argiro family, and both had the idea to help coal miners find a meal they could take underground that was hearty, wouldn't spoil, and was compact enough to fit into lunch boxes. John Brunett added that they are content knowing that their grandfather started making pepperoni rolls in the thirties, when they all started being made: "Nobody really knows who started it, and we never really thought it was worth the fight. We are the oldest bakery, and we know we are one of the originators."

Tomaro's Bakery, whose slogan is "Eat Tomaro's Bread Today," was opened in 1914 by Brunett's great-grandfather, Antonio Carmen Tomaro. Not

Above: Tomaro's Bakery is the oldest Italian bakery in West Virginia. Image Credit: Tomaro's Bakery.

only is Tomaro's the oldest Italian bakery in West Virginia, but it also has been passed through the family for four generations, making it the longest-run family-bakery business in the state. After Antonio Carmen Tomaro's death, the bakery was passed to his daughter, Anna Tomaro Brunett, and her husband John Brunett (namesake of the current owner). When John Brunett passed away unexpectedly, their son Sam continued to operate the bakery with his mother. The current owner John Brunett credits his father Sam with modernization of the facilities to increase production. If John's children decide to take over the bakery, they will carry on the family tradition of baking Italian bread and pepperoni rolls into the fifth generation.

When the bakery opened, Marisa said, her great-grandfather used to just bake bread; he delivered the hot loaves in a basket all around Clarksburg. For the bakery's recent hundredth anniversary, the family found and displayed that bread basket as part of the celebration, along with the world's largest pepperoni roll—that they know of, at least. They baked six seven-foot pepperoni rolls, which were documented, measured, and photographed with hopes of ending up in the *Guinness Book of World Records*.

Tomaro's touts that its roll is unlike others because of its secret ingredients. "It's like the Coke recipe, hidden in a vault," Marisa said. Marisa claimed that the ingredients added to Tomaro's roll make it last

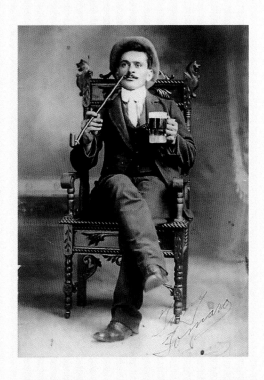

Above right: Antonio Carmen Tomaro, of Abruzzo, Italy, started the bakery in 1914. Image Credit: Tomaro's Bakery. Right: Sam Brunett took over operation of Tomaro's Bakery with his mother Anna Tomaro Brunett at just eighteen years old. The two are pictured here together, sometime later, in 1980. Image Credit: Tomaro's Bakery.

MEMORIES

April Kaull

"My first pepperoni rolls were those made from scratch in the Wallace Elementary School kitchen. I can remember watching the cooks rolling the dough and cutting the sticks of pepperoni as we sat in the cafeteria early in morning after the bus dropped us off. Later, as a young reporter on the go in North Central West Virginia, a fresh-from-the-oven pepperoni roll from Tomaro's Bakery was truly a taste of almost heaven. By the way, Tomaro's pepperoni rolls are also made with sticks, which may be why I love them best. Or it might be as simple as this, 'the best pepperoni roll is the one you grew up with—the one that you'll keep coming home for.'"

—April Kaull, a Clarksburg, WV, native and longtime TV news anchor

Previous page, top: The Tomaro's Bakery pepperoni roll contains a few sticks of pepperoni. Previous page, bottom: The Tomaro's pepperoni roll is composed of an Italian dough and sticks of spicy pepperoni. Tomaro's also sells pizza shells, hoagie buns, and more. Below: Current owner John Brunett's grandfather, also named John Brunett, rolls dough at Tomaro's Bakery alongside Tommy G. Ketroh and John Tiano. Image Credit: Tomaro's Bakery. Below right: Sam Brunett is credited with modernization of Tomaro's Bakery, which led to an increase in production. Image Credit: Tomaro's Bakery.

longer, taste better, and look less pale. "We've stayed true to our recipe since day one. We haven't changed it up." The final product is more square than most, with a crustier Italian dough and stuffed with sticks of spicy meat, each packed to look perfect. Years ago, when people began stuffing pepperoni rolls with cheese, John's father looked into it. "He found out you would have to use a synthetic cheese to make it shelf stable, and he said he wasn't going to do that," John said. "You're basically selling flavored plastic. If you leave a natural cheese out on the counter for two days—without it being refrigerated—it would

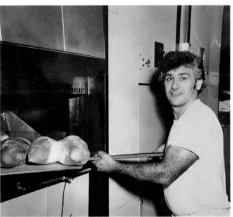

grow a beard, so it has to be a synthetic-type cheese, and we want our product to stay natural and original."

Tomaro's is onto something with its consistency: in 2015, *Southern Living* named Tomaro's Bakery's pepperoni rolls as one of "The South's Best Cheap Eats Under $10," and Marisa said fans from near and far travel to buy them. "People will come up and just get bags upon bags upon bags to take with them," she said. "It's people who have lived here and miss the pepperoni roll. They grew up eating these."

John Brunett, named after his grandfather who was the second-generation owner, is a fourth-generation owner. His mother Janice and sister Marisa are co-owners.

But tradition hasn't stymied product development, according to John. "When my sister-in-law had her kids, Dad would get mad because they wouldn't eat the entire pepperoni roll," he said. So, Sam started using spare dough to roll mini ones. "They're definitely a big hit," John said, and not only with those who have smaller bellies. They're especially popular during football season, served with marinara, or maybe peppers. Caterers also use them as hors d'oeuvres.

Tomaro's has gone bigger as well: the bakery's general manager, Steve Shartinger, said many locally owned restaurants and sports bars in Fairmont serve Tomaro's pepperoni rolls. "We sell them to restaurants that use them with peppers and cheese or chili and cheese," John said. Some of the restaurants even get a special roll that Tomaro's calls "double-stuff": a six-ounce pepperoni roll twice the size of the regular.

For those who have moved, Tomaro's ships to all fifty states within one to two days through its website: http://www.annasofglenelk.com/, named after John and Marisa's grandmother.

MEMORIES   *Alexis McMillen*

Alexis McMillen, a native of Clarksburg, WV, said of Tomaro's Bakery, "When I was growing up in Clarksburg, sometimes on the weekends, my uncle Mark would bring us fresh rolls still warm from the oven in a white paper bag. There wasn't (and still isn't) quite anything that's so good. It made me feel proud of being Italian, lucky to live somewhere that we could get such delicious artisan bread, and growing up there, we all knew it was something special that not everyone had. It's true for many of us. . . . Pepperoni rolls are the true taste of home!"

18

D'ANNUNZIO'S ITALIAN BREAD
(THE HEALTH BREAD COMPANY)
1909 WILLIAMS AVE.
CLARKSBURG, WV 26301
304-622-3492
—
D'ANNUNZIO'S ITALIAN BAKERY
115 SURFRIDER BLVD.
LONGS, SC 29568
843-390-1919
DANNUNZIOSBREAD.COM

D'Annunzio's Italian Bread (*The Health Bread Company*)

In Clarksburg, in the world of pepperoni rolls, people often pledge their allegiance to one of the two old-school Italian bakery giants: Tomaro's in the Glen Elk neighborhood or D'Annunzio's in the North View side of town. "I've heard it all my life," said Chris D'Annunzio, who owns D'Annunzio's Italian Bread with his brother Rick. "People say Tomaro's is the best or D'Annunzio's is the best. I've heard it ever since I was a kid growing up in the bakery. Some like your stuff on this end, but they hate you on this end," he said, showing Clarksburg's pepperoni roll division with a swipe of his hands.

D'Annunzio's was started in 1931 by Chris and Rick's great-grandfather, whose family had been in the baking business in Italy. He enlisted help from his son-in-law, who was originally a contractor, and it's been passed down the line. Now, with Chris and Rick, who took over the bakery after their father, Ben, the business sits in the hands of fourth-generation owners. And, as the brothers mull retirement, it could soon be with the fifth generation.

As demonstrated by the bakery's lineage, family, heritage, and community are important to the D'Annunzios. Chris credits the success of the bakery to the support from its beginnings in the Italian neighborhood and community in North View. "It's the people who build your bakery," Chris said. "You present your

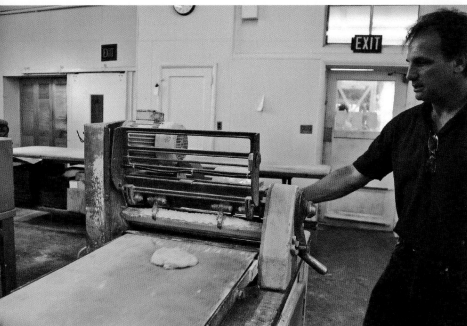

Opposite: D'Annunzio's Italian Bread is located in the Northview neighborhood of Clarksburg, WV.

Left: D'Annunzio's focuses on using a harder Italian crust for its pepperoni rolls.

Lower left: Chris D'Annunzio and his brother Rick co-own D'Annunzio's Italian Bread.

MEMORIES

Erin Blake

Clarksburg, WV, native Erin Blake's memories of visiting her grandparents with her brother in the North View neighborhood revolve around one thing: D'Annunzio's. "To me pepperoni rolls just remind me of family.... My grandparents lived a street up from D'Annunzio's. I remember walking down there holding my grandma's hand, and later my brother and °I running ahead while she yelled to us to stay out of the street," she said. "Later we were allowed to go ourselves. There's nothing better than those fresh baked rolls straight out of the oven. We knew the workers, we knew the owners, and it just always felt like a special experience. Even when I've taken my nephew, I felt like a tradition was being passed on. Seeing a D'Annunzio's bag still brings a smile to my face."

product. It's our heritage; it's our life. We were a product of the times and made a living being Italian people when nobody wanted to buy from Italians. But the Italian community rallied around us."

First located on Williams Avenue in a brick building with a leased oven, D'Annunzio's began as The Health Bread Company, selling Italian and French bread with "The Essential Health Builder" written on the bag. When, in the 1970s, the federal government objected that the bakery claimed to be healthy, the company changed its name. About a decade earlier, the bakery had also changed locations—but it didn't go far, settling permanently across the street at 1909 Williams Avenue, where it stands today. The bricks that make up the building were bought for fifteen dollars—the remnants of another bakery in town that had been torn down.

The brothers, who had watched the construction of the new bakery, grew up helping in different capacities. Chris became the baker of the family, while Rick played the role of mechanic. Chris, who now considers himself to be a specialty baker, was learning how to make pepperoni rolls before he could see any of the machines that towered high above him. As a teenager, he scrubbed racks to help keep up with demand. At that age, Chris had already bought into the lifestyle of a family business: "I've not been off one Sunday since I was nineteen years old," he said. "We're a professional bakery; it's been drilled into me. I get up and come to work for it. It's the respect of the other workers and the people who are here." Now, the bakery runs eighteen hours a day with a twenty-person staff.

Even though D'Annunzio's is in the bread business—selling hard-crust Italian bread, soft-crust Italian bread, a home loaf, pizza shells, hoagie buns, and hamburger buns—they're really known for their pepperoni rolls. "I would have to say we're the number-one pepperoni roll guys around," Chris said. "They can all claim fame, but ain't nobody made more pepperoni rolls in the state of West Virginia than Chris D'Annunzio. I've been the head baker here since I was a kid—since we had a guy work for my dad for forty-three years. When he died, I was the man. And I'm still making pepperoni rolls."

For its rolls, D'Annunzio's uses a harder Italian crust with stick pepperoni. One staff person is fully devoted to cutting the meat. Like the building and the recipe, much of the equipment is decades old, including the mixer, large tubs for dough, dividing machines, and

Opposite: D'Annunzio's Italian Bread uses a hard, Italian dough paired with spicy sticks of pepperoni to make its famous pepperoni rolls.

Above: D'Annunzio's Italian Bread focuses on being an Italian bakery first and foremost, which includes selling bread, buns, crusts, and more. D'Annunzio's Italian Bread was previously named The Health Bread Company. Because the original name indicated there was a health benefit from the bread, which the federal government objected to, the bakery now operates as D'Annunzio's Italian Bread (The Health Bread Company).

MEMORIES

Kayla Poling

"No Poling family vacation is complete without a batch of my mom's pepperoni rolls for the car ride! As far as buying pepperoni rolls, D'Annunzio's are my fave! You haven't had the true West Virginia experience until you've made the trek to their bakery in Clarksburg for a straight-out-of-the-oven pepperoni roll! If it's more of an entree pepperoni roll you crave then Colasessano's in Fairmont has the best! I've taken the 'long way' back to Wetzel County on many Friday nights so I could pick up a few to share with the family!"

—Kayla Poling, a native of Reader, WV

molding machines. Chris grabs a ball of dough and adds a piece of stick pepperoni. "Then you add two more on this side, turn it over, and roll—right there is your pepperoni roll," he said. Most of D'Annunzio's pepperoni rolls have three pieces of pepperoni. He digs through the pepperoni pile to find sticks that are on the slim side. "See, now these ones, we would add more—because I don't cheat. If I didn't give you enough, that's cheating you. I want you to enjoy this product." Consistency is key.

"It's a lot of hard work, lots of damn hard work, lots of sweat," Chris said of his profession. "We came to make a living and go home, but you never get to go home because the bakery becomes part of your life. Through arguments, happy times, good things, notoriety—that's us, and that has been us for years."

Chris's commitment has not only benefited his own bakery; it has contributed to the culinary culture of West Virginia. "Will the pepperoni roll catch on eventually? Damn right it will," Chris said. "Just like you're going to Boston and eating a lobster. Steamed crabs in Maryland. Maybe a good steak in Texas, I don't know. When you come to West Virginia, you are going to eat a pepperoni roll."

The bakery sees many of the same customers day after day, plus new ones who always trickle in from out of town. Like Tomaro's, its double pepperoni roll ends up in some restaurants, which stack them with cheese and peppers. D'Annunzio's pepperoni rolls can be found in all major grocery stores in North Central West Virginia, and the bakery also has a presence in Myrtle Beach, SC, run by Chris's brother Steve.

Above left: When it's not possible to devour hot pepperoni rolls fresh from the oven, packaged ones from D'Annunzio's Italian Bread are also available, which are perfect for transport and consumption later on.

Left: D'Annunzio's Italian Bread produces many, many pepperoni rolls five days per week: Sunday, Monday, Wednesday, Thursday, and Friday.

RR 19
GYPSY, WV 26361
304-592-0461

Abruzzino's Italian Bakery

When Chris Abruzzino opened Abruzzino's Italian Bakery in Gypsy, WV, on March 5, 1985, he was the newcomer to the pepperoni roll business. Just twenty years old and with a new baby, Abruzzino was looking to build a steady source of income. Situated between Fairmont and Clarksburg, he knew there was a market for his idea: a traditional pepperoni roll, but with a twist—soft bread.

Abruzzino had grown up working at Marty's Bakery, a local bakery known for its pepperoni rolls, just down the road along Route 19 (the bakery burned down in 1994). From ages thirteen to nineteen, he learned the ins and outs of the business. "I was young and full of energy," Abruzzino said. "As a vendor, I had worked out on the road, and when people would come buy bread up at Marty's, they would say, 'This is really good bread, but . . .' I just kept hearing 'but, but, but'—'It's really good, but two days later it's no good.' Or 'It tastes all right, but it's tough, it's dry, it's hard.' That stuck in my head, and I knew there was a niche." It was time for something new.

Although he grew up on Italian bread, Abruzzino knew that's not what customers wanted anymore, so he found bakery equipment for sale in the newspaper. That's when he started his bakery. His bread differs from everybody else's in the local bread market because it combines the traditional Italian product with some of the softness of a typical white sandwich bread. "When I first started," Abruzzino said, "everything in this area was the Italian

Left: Abruzzino's Italian Bakery is a newer bakery compared to others in the region, but it made a name for itself early on with its fresh take on the traditional pepperoni roll.

bread with no preservatives. It's pretty dry and pretty crusty. It's tasty, but it's not good for two or three days down the road." That's just the natural texture of traditional Italian bread, he said. But as new people were coming to the Clarksburg area, Abruzzino kept hearing the same comments. His recipe blend melds old-world and new-world styles of bread. "I felt like the market needed this type of bread, and I wanted to bring it," he said.

But the older bakeries in the area saw the different bread as straying from the traditional pepperoni roll. "I was the brand-new guy with a totally different product than they had because of the bread," he said. "I was early twenties, and all these older guys fifty-plus would say, 'Ah, boy, you'll never make it,' or 'He's making that white bread, that will

Below: Abruzzino's Italian Bakery offers a soft white-bread pepperoni roll with sliced pepperoni that can come stuffed with yellow American cheese or hot-pepper cheese.

Above: Abruzzino's Italian Bakery churns out three thousand pepperoni rolls per day.

never work.' And it's so funny now, thirty years later, many are buying 'soft bread' sticky labels to put on their pepperoni roll packages. The market changed, time has changed, people changed."

A few years after Abruzzino's Italian Bakery started, Abruzzino once again strayed from the traditional roll, switching from stick pepperoni to the new sliced pepperoni. The cost was the biggest reason, Abruzzino said. But another benefit is that the circles of pepperoni are cut thinner than Abruzzino can cut them, which enables them to spread throughout the dough so that pepperoni grease can permeate the whole roll. "A lot of folks look at the bottom of the roll to see if it's all saturated with grease," he said, "that's how some people buy a pepperoni roll."

Around the same time Abruzzino switched to sliced pepperoni, he also started adding cheese to the pepperoni rolls. "Supply and demand was probably the key to getting into the cheese-pepperoni-roll business. People wanted it," Abruzzino said. Abruzzino's sells a plain pepperoni roll, a pepperoni roll with yellow American cheese, and a hot-pepper-cheese roll in two sizes, three ounces and six ounces.

The ten-person bakery staff produces three thousand pepperoni rolls per day. The biggest seller is the American cheese roll. The convenience- and grocery-store market for Abruzzino's products stretches from Morgantown, WV, to Flatwoods, Parkersburg, and Grafton. Many retail customers have been coming on the same day for thirty years. "On Sundays, we know what folks we're going to have in here, and if today is Thursday, we know we're going to have so-and-so," he said. "With God and good luck and hard work, we've found our niche and help keep some of the tradition alive."

Left: Chris Abruzzino opened up Abruzzino's Italian Bakery when he was just twenty years old.

Below left: Abruzzino's sells a plain pepperoni roll, a pepperoni roll with yellow American cheese, and a hot-pepper-cheese pepperoni roll in two sizes, three ounces and six ounces.

407 BEECHURST AVE
MORGANTOWN, WV 26505
304-292-9433
CHICOBAKERY.COM

Chico Bakery—Home of Julia's Pepperoni Rolls

Chico Bakery in Morgantown, WV, is defined by its pepperoni rolls—so much so that it's often followed up with its tagline, "Home of Julia's Pepperoni Rolls."

But who is Julia?

This is a story of a son's love and good taste.

Samuel Chico Sr. founded Chico Dairy Company as a dairy and ice-cream parlor with a side bakery business that offered bread, cake, cookies, and doughnuts—a natural accompaniment to the dairy products. It wasn't until Sam Chico Jr. took over that the bakery began making pepperoni rolls—Sam thought his mother Julia's recipe was too good not to share beyond their family. The pepperoni roll Chico's bakes today is based on the same recipe Julia herself began baking at home in 1925.

"Mrs. Chico made the mix, the dough we use right now. We've modernized it and put it into production," said Chico Bakery supervisor Gary Miller. "Her pepperoni rolls were different from any of the others in the area because most people were using the crusty, hard bread, but hers is a softer, sweeter pepperoni roll. That's what sets us apart from the competitors." Miller said that a lot of other bakeries have tried to duplicate it, but no one has fully succeeded: "You know, imitation is the highest form of flattery."

Left: Chico Bakery is the home of Julia's Pepperoni Rolls, which can be found in stores across the state.

MEMORIES *Lenna Walkup*

"My mom always made pepperoni rolls with homemade bread dough stuffed with pepperoni and cheese. It was a staple growing up, especially for lunch, probably partially because there were so many of us and it was easy (and inexpensive) to make pepperoni rolls in bulk. As I got older, they were my go-to lunch or snack on the way to soccer games in high school because they weren't too heavy. I always just assumed that they were everywhere and was surprised to learn when I went to college that the out-of-staters had never heard of them (especially surprised when I moved to Florida for grad school and they were nowhere to be found!)."

—Lenna Walkup, a native of Buckeye, WV

Above right: Chico Bakery can produce up to ten thousand pepperoni rolls per day.

Right: Julia's Pepperoni Rolls contain sliced pepperoni and the choice of fresh Sargento provolone cheese, hot-pepper cheese, or double stuffed.

In 1968, the bakery part of the business was growing and needed a larger location and new equipment to accommodate the demand of customers. It's been at its 407 Beechurst Avenue location ever since. As the business grew and evolved—expanding the company into Chico Enterprises, Inc.—the bakery's focus narrowed. Today, under the current president and CEO Samuel A. Chico III, Chico Bakery is the nation's largest producer of pepperoni rolls, churning out about seven thousand to ten thousand a day, with a maximum capacity of around three thousand cases per week. With twenty-four rolls in each case, that's seventy-two thousand pepperoni rolls per week, which end up everywhere from Detroit, MI, to Buffalo, NY, to Erie, PA, to the Carolinas—ten states in all.

West Virginia University in Morgantown is one of the bakery's biggest customers: Chico is its official provider not only for campus events but also for game-day crowds at both the Milan Puskar Stadium during football season and at the WVU Coliseum during basketball season.

Chico Bakery is represented at baseball games now too, as a sponsor

Below left, center, and right: Chico Bakery has invested in machinery to help increase product output, while many other bakeries still roll by hand. Today, Chico Bakery can produce seventy-two thousand pepperoni rolls per week—which then are shipped all over the country. Regionally, Chico Bakery Julia's Pepperoni Rolls can be found in grocery stores, Dairy Marts, Par Mar stores, BFS stores, and more.

of the West Virginia Black Bears, Morgantown's minor-league baseball team affiliated with the Pittsburgh Pirates.

Chico Bakery sells three kinds of rolls: pepperoni and provolone cheese, pepperoni and hot-pepper cheese, and double-stuffed pepperoni. "The original pepperoni roll was just pepperoni and bread. And after we started adding cheeses to it, the sales for the regular pepperoni roll just dropped drastically," Miller said. So they created the double-stuffed pepperoni roll: two ounces of pepperoni in a 5.5-ounce roll. One-third of the sandwich is meat. The cheese version is stuffed with one ounce of either Sargento provolone or hot-pepper cheese and one ounce of pepperoni.

"We don't advertise it, because we don't have a traditional storefront," Miller said, "but anybody who walks in can buy pepperoni rolls for the same

COMMUNITY

"On Friday, I have three or four food-kitchen pickups. It bugs me that manufacturers can throw away stuff that could help feed someone else. There are people who go to bed in 2016 hungry."

—Gary Miller, supervisor of Chico's Bakery, gives second-quality stock to food pantries in Marion, Monongalia, and Preston Counties every week price our grocery suppliers buy it for. We can sell you one roll, or we can sell you one hundred cases." Miller said they have a lot of people who go through the area at lunchtime and stop in for whatever rolls are fresh.

Pepperoni rolls are also available for purchase online at http://www.chicobakery.com/cart/, a good option for people who want to send the pepperoni rolls to relatives in the military. Chico's ships the pepperoni rolls frozen domestically, and they arrive frozen; they last 180 days. If refrigerated, the pepperoni rolls last for twenty-eight days, and at room temperature, they're good for about a week. Chico Bakery doesn't ship internationally because they don't want to risk compromising the freshness of their product.

But even if they are fresh, not every roll comes out perfect enough to package, either because of a machine or a human error. The pepperoni rolls that don't pass quality control are boxed up and given to local food kitchens. "On Friday, I have three or four food-kitchen pickups," Miller said. He tries to spread the pepperoni rolls around Monongalia, Preston, and Marion Counties. "It bugs me that manufacturers can throw away stuff that could help feed someone else. There are people who go to bed in 2016 hungry," he said. "We want to try to help that."

506 PENNSYLVANIA AVE.
FAIRMONT, WV 26554
304-363-9713
—
141 MIDDLETOWN CIRCLE
FAIRMONT, WV 26554
304-363-0571
WWW.COLASESSANOS.COM

Colasessano's World Famous Pizza & Pepperoni Buns

Decades after a handful of local bakeries clamored to be the first to produce hot, fluffy pepperoni rolls, another bakery looked to perfect them. Colasessano's World Famous Pizza & Pepperoni Buns in Fairmont took the pepperoni roll; sliced it down the center; and added sauce, cheese, and Oliverio Italian Style peppers (hot, sweet, or mixed) to make a full meal. Here, the roll is called a "bun," for reasons no one recalls. But the name has stuck. "Everybody in Fairmont knows Colasessano's, and it's the place to go," said John Menas, who owns "Colo's" with his wife, Carrie. Colasessano's is the only major producer with a restaurant, and most of its pepperoni buns are consumed on-site.

Filippo Colasessano, who began the business in 1919, had been a coal miner. After he lost his leg in a mining accident, the coal company sold him a building on Pennsylvania Avenue, which he turned into a company store and, later, added a bar that sold hot dogs. Filippo ran the business until his death in 1957, when his son, "Spider," and Spider's wife, Josephine, took over and began selling pizza. Colasessano's still has its original location.

"Here's how it was told to me," Menas said: "Josephine and her mother lived in Buffalo, NY. Filippo and Filomena Colasessano and their son John, aka Spider, lived in Fairmont. I'm sure their families knew each other over in Italy, but how they got split up in this country, I do not know. I was told it was an

Left: Colasessano's World Famous Pizza & Pepperoni Buns is not only a bakery, but also a restaurant.

arranged marriage between Spider and Josephine. And when Josephine came from Buffalo to Fairmont, they brought the pizza recipe with them," Menas said.

When the couple added pizza to the store and ended up with leftover dough, they started making pepperoni buns. After baking the bun, they added cheese, then some canned peppers, then some hot-dog sauce on a whim. "They didn't have a certain size that they made. They would mix up 150 pounds of dough at a time, throw it up on the table, and six women would just grab it and whack off a piece and start rolling a bun," Menas said. The reception was astounding.

And then tragedy struck.

Spider died of a heart attack in 1973 at age forty-four. Afterward, the store went to carry out only under the operation of Josephine and their son Joey. Some days, Menas said, when there was a football game, they would be sold out of pizzas by 2 or 3 p.m.

Menas, like the founding Colasessano, had worked in mining. After thirty years with Consol Energy, he was operating a convenience store on Route 19 when a Pepsi delivery man mentioned that Joey Colasessano was looking to sell the restaurant. Though Menas is of Croatian descent, not Italian, he grew up eating at Colasessano's World Famous Pizza & Pepperoni Buns.

"I said, 'You don't sell Colasessano's. That's a family business. It'll be in the family forever,'" Menas said. "I told him that if Joey is seriously looking to sell, send him my way." Two days later, Joey walked in and Menas "just about died."

On April 1, 2003, John and Carrie Menas purchased Colasessano's. To

MEMORIES

Marion Ohlinger

"For three years I lived a block above the original Colasessano's in a punk house we affectionately called the Dewey Street Home for Wayward Musicians. I ate a pepperoni roll every day, as they were only $2.20 back then. Many days they were the only thing I ate all day, and a lot of days the only thing anyone in that house ate all day. I like to think that Colasessano's saved my life, because I would have starved without that big cheap pepperoni roll."

—Marion Ohlinger, chef of
Hill & Hollow in Morgantown, WV

Oliverio Peppers

Oliverio Italian Style Peppers is a family-owned business in Clarksburg that produces peppers (in sauce or brine), cauliflower, garden mix, and more. Local bakeries in North Central West Virginia often carry jars of the peppers in sauce alongside pepperoni rolls.

ensure consistency and customer satisfaction, the couple ran the business the exact same way as the Colasessanos had for one year—opening at 8 a.m., closing at 6 p.m., and shutting down the restaurant for three weeks for vacations. After the year was up, the restaurant expanded the hours and the menu and allowed employees to take vacations when they wanted, provided enough people were available to cover for them.

"If you would have told me when I was younger, 'One of these days, you are going to be a baker. You are going to be real interested in making dough and learning all about it,' I would have said you have to be nuts," Menas said. "I would have said, 'I'm a coal miner. I run a fifty-ton locomotive underground. I haul coal. I love it, and I'll never do that.' And just like that . . . it all changed."

The recipe remains intact: fresh-baked buns filled with five or six strips of stick pepperoni baked to golden-brown perfection then slathered with optional provolone cheese; the original meat sauce; and sweet, mixed, or hot Oliverio Peppers. "The bun is so much bigger than anybody else's in the market," Menas explained. "You get sauce, cheese, peppers loaded up. With most buns, you don't get that. You just get a regular pepperoni roll."

Colasessano's makes about one thousand buns a day, six days per week. They're closed on Sundays because Menas said he worked too many Sundays when he was in the mines. These days, customers order fairly equal amounts of both the pizza and the pepperoni buns. The most popular bun, Menas said—which happens to be his favorite as well—is the one with just cheese and sauce.

John and Carrie kept most of the menu items, including the pizza and the "Spider Special," which is a fresh-toasted hoagie filled with salami; provolone

cheese; and mild, mixed, or hot peppers on a round bun. The only item from the previous menu that has been discontinued was a hot dog served with provolone cheese, and the only minor change in the original bun recipe was swapping the type of flour. Previously, Colasessano's used Robin Hood Flour, which comes from Canada and was easier to get for Josephine's recipe when she was in Buffalo. During an incident in which the flour couldn't be purchased because it hadn't cleared customs, Menas took steps to avoid future disruptions by partnering with General Mills, which crafted a nearly identical flour blend—containing the same amount of

Above: Colasessano's refers to its pepperoni roll as a pepperoni bun, and it makes about one thousand buns per day.

Above: The Colasessano's pepperoni bun can be served split down the center, drizzled with sauce, cheese, and Oliverio Peppers.

gluten and other ingredients. Colasessano's World Famous Pizza & Pepperoni Buns now uses this flour for all of its products.

The couple's other changes include an expanded menu, turning the business into a full-scale sit-down restaurant, and an additional location near the Middletown Mall. For about three years, Colasessano's also had a restaurant in Morgantown, where its buns were named the best pepperoni roll by *Morgantown Magazine* in 2012 and 2013. "When we went to Morgantown, we took off like a barn on fire for about three months," Menas said. Then, due to the temporary closure of the Cheat Lake bridge, business died off and didn't return once the bridge reopened. "Once people get set in their ways with how they travel, they tend to stay on that route."

The original location on Pennsylvania Avenue has hosted and been frequented by the likes of former Sen. Ted Kennedy; Alabama football coach Nick Saban from nearby Monongah; famed basketball coaches Rick Pitino, Bob Huggins, and Billy Donovan; retired professional wrestler Dominic DeNucci; and countless West Virginia politicians and leaders, many of whom have photos hung on the walls from their visits. Another favorite photo in the Pennsylvania Avenue location shows Spider Colasessano guarding Air Force One when former President Lyndon B. Johnson flew into West Virginia. The building is now slated for a remodel. "We are going to build a new store right beside that one on Pennsylvania Avenue and remodel it. Nice stone in the front, nice windows, and a nice metal roof," Menas said. "There's a lot of history in that old building. If that building could talk, I would hate to see what all could come out of there."

If bun lovers are unable to venture out to one of the two Fairmont locations, another option exists: Menas ships his pepperoni buns and pizzas around the country, which started when his son, who was stationed with the military in Los Angeles, was craving Colasessano's. "He wanted a Colasessano's pizza so bad he was ready to fly home to get one," Menas said. Menas told his son that he couldn't ship a frozen pizza made of raw dough because it would arrive raw and no longer in its signature rectangular form. But he had a solution.

Menas made two pepperoni buns and pizzas with only sauce and

MEMORIES

Ben Adducchio

Ben Adducchio, a Fairmont, WV, native, who works as an actor in New York City, said, "I only get to eat them twice a year—I absolutely positively must have a Colasessano's pepperoni roll when I'm in West Virginia. My trip is not complete without one!"

MEMORIES
Rocco Muriale

"I have a lot of memories of pepperoni rolls from childhood. . . . I can remember my grandparents making them. I can remember little local bakeries. . . . There's still Tomaro's . . . and I can remember Tiano's in Glen Elk and D'Annunzio's in North View. As a child in the Glen Elk neighborhood, we would go up to the one bakery in one of the alleys, and I think they would sell us and heat up, for a couple pennies, like two-day-old pepperoni rolls. When they'd give them to us hot, it tasted like fine dining to us at that age. . . . At the restaurant, we do a pepperoni hoagie. We don't do the traditional pepperoni roll in a bun like all the other places. We just do our own little twist on it, and we put the pepperoni and some sauce and put it on a hoagie bun, bake it, and serve it fresh and hot. We don't remake; we just put a little different spin on it."

—Rocco Muriale,
owner of Muriale's in Fairmont, WV

pepperoni, baked them, and then took them out of the pan to cool down. Then, he flash-froze them, put them in a plastic bag, and placed them in a shipping container with ice packs. "He called me one night and said 'You will never believe where I am at,'" Menas said. "He said 'I'm at Colasessano's.'" Menas's son thawed the pizzas and buns in the refrigerator, placed them in the oven for five minutes to heat up, added cheese to both, and then heated them up for another five minutes. It was just like home.

That's when Menas began shipping pizzas and buns all over. On one particular day, Menas shipped an order to Houston, Texas, which would arrive within twenty-four hours. "We get a lot of people who get on our website or hear about us and just want to try it," Menas said.

Colasessano's pepperoni buns can also be found at Little General Stores in the area and most of the Hometown Hot Dogs locations, which sell a slightly smaller-sized pepperoni bun. Local restaurants Woody's and Att's, both known for their hot dogs, sell the Colasessano's pepperoni bun filled with their own hot-dog sauce.

In the near future, Menas hopes to produce a tiny version: a small ball of dough with a piece of pepperoni stuck through it. "People will put a bag on the seat of their truck and pop one in their mouth every now and then," he said, noting that they seem to be a big seller at other bakeries.

And as far as the future for his family? Menas hopes his kids will take over the business and start a new family lineage, although he acknowledges that it's a lot of hard work and early mornings. "Sometimes if somebody calls off, we have to stay and do that job. I'm the dishwasher a lot," Menas said. "But it's still better than going underground at midnight."

Rogers and Mazza's Italian Bakery (Marty's Bakery)

624 PHILIPPI PIKE
CLARKSBURG, WV 26301
304-622-6682
WWW.PEPPERONIROLLS.NET
TWITTER: @PEPPERONIROLL

Rogers and Mazza's Italian Bakery bridges the old and the new. The bakery, which was created in 1996, brings two brands under the same roof: one that caters to the traditional pepperoni roll crowd, and another that bakes outside the box.

Marty's Bakery was a Clarksburg staple that had been serving pepperoni rolls since the 1950s. When it burned down in 1994, Steve Rogers, who ran several local convenience stores, purchased the place. Shortly after, his stepsons Dennis and Michael Mazza joined the business. "Marty [DeFazio] came to me even before it burnt down and wanted me to take it over," Rogers said, "and I just wasn't interested." But following the fire, Marty's daughter, who was an attorney, approached Rogers. She said she had no intentions of reopening the bakery herself, but her dad wanted her to work out an agreement with Rogers for him to use the Marty's name and build a bakery.

On March 26, 1996, Steve opened up Rogers and Mazza's Italian Bakery in a new location along Philippi Pike in Clarksburg—just down the road from where Marty's

Above: From left to right: Dennis Mazza, Steve Rogers, and Michael Mazza co-own Rogers and Mazza's Italian Bakery. Rogers is the stepfather to the Mazza brothers.

Left: Marty's Bakery was a Clarksburg staple that had been serving pepperoni rolls since the 1950s. It burned down in 1994, but Rogers and Mazza's Italian Bakery still carry the rolls' recipe.

Bakery used to be. The bakery began by selling Marty's traditional Italian-bread pepperoni rolls with pepperoni sticks. "We started making only about sixty-dozen pepperoni rolls a day, but then, we decided that so many companies were making bread around here that we wanted to specialize in the pepperoni rolls," Rogers said. He began a Rogers and Mazza's line of products, including a new take on the pepperoni roll, in 1998.

"I was in the convenience-store business, so I already had a recipe for a nontraditional type of pepperoni roll," Rogers said. "They're not Italian based; they have a sweeter taste to them." In contrast to the traditional Marty's roll, the Rogers and Mazza's pepperoni roll uses a sweeter dough, developed through trial and error, and sliced pepperoni (instead of sticks). It comes in three different varieties: plain, mozzarella, or hot-pepper cheese. These each come in six-ounce or three-ounce sizes. Mini pepperoni rolls come in plain or with mozzarella cheese.

Dennis Mazza said that the Clarksburg area has always been partial to the traditional stick pepperoni, like the Marty's roll, but when they expanded beyond the area, they noticed that those customers preferred sliced pepperoni, which is a bit spicier. Michael Mazza said that the slices allow the grease to flavor the roll better: "People like the grease."

And despite claims that sliced pepperoni is of inferior quality, Rogers assures it is not. "It really is the same. You get them in long sticks, and it comes prewrapped with a string at the end of it. The only difference is how you slice it," Rogers said. And whether it's stick or slice, it's always Hormel.

Even with the development of its own line of pepperoni rolls, Rogers and Mazza's has continued to sell the traditional Marty-style rolls—partly as an homage to Marty's historical influence on pepperoni rolls in Clarksburg, and partly as a fulfillment of demand. When they began, the Marty's side of the business was huge, but gradually the focus shifted as the Rogers and Mazza's version caught on. Now, Rogers and Mazza's produces more than twenty thousand per day, with 99 percent of the business coming from the Rogers and Mazza's pepperoni roll. The large mozzarella-cheese roll is the best seller.

"We began adding mozzarella to get that pizza flavor," Dennis said. "People like pizza, and that cheese with the pepperoni makes for a good roll." For those who like a spicier pepperoni roll, the hot-pepper cheese is available. "Adding the cheese makes it like a complete meal," Rogers said.

Regularly shipping to cities across West Virginia, including Charleston, Beckley, Huntington, and Logan, and distributing to about 650 stores in state, Rogers and Mazza's takes credit for pushing the pepperoni roll beyond North Central West Virginia. Pittsburgh is also a growing market. Of course, the Pennsylvania city has bakeries, but none are dedicated to the pepperoni roll. "We don't want it to just be a state secret anymore; we want it to go nationwide," Michael said. Rolls have been shipped to all fifty states and soldiers on duty overseas.

Above: The Marty's Italian Pepperoni Roll is a traditional Italian bread with sticks of pepperoni.

Above right: The Rogers and Mazza's pepperoni roll is made with a sweet dough and sliced pepperoni and comes in three different varieties: plain, mozzarella, or hot-pepper cheese. Each variety comes in six ounces or three ounces. The store also produces mini pepperoni rolls, plain or with mozzarella cheese.

Right: Rogers and Mazza's has worked to push the pepperoni roll outside North Central West Virginia and into all corners of the state, and even beyond.

This kind of distribution didn't happen overnight. "When I started here in 1997," Dennis said, "[Rogers] gave me the van and said to go, and I went to Charleston. People hardly knew what pepperoni rolls were." Dennis said that pepperoni rolls weren't being sold down there yet; if people knew about them, they were homemade. The market was so bad, Rogers and Mazza's almost pulled out like some of its competitors. "But we gave it some time and stuck with it," Dennis said. Charleston is now one of the highest-selling regions.

As the bakery continues to grow, the owners know they will continue to experiment with new products, different recipes, and tasty additions. "We've had marinara sauce and a sweet-pepper spread," Dennis said. They're considering other cured meats like sausage and salami too: "I've tried baking a roll with summer sausage, and it was great," according to Dennis. More health-conscious versions, like turkey pepperoni or wheat bread, are possibilities as well. "There's so much more room to grow," Rogers said. "There's no end to it."

Far left: Rogers and Mazza's most popular roll is the large mozzarella-cheese pepperoni roll.

Left: Rogers and Mazza's began adding cheese to its own line of pepperoni rolls in order to make it a more satisfying meal.

128 S. THIRD STREET
CLARKSBURG, WV 26301
304-623-3384

Home Industry Bakery (A&M Bakery)

Home Industry Bakery pepperoni roll lovers know which color bag to pick up at their local convenience store: red writing for the traditional, purple if they want some provolone cheese, or green for the hot-cheese fanatic.

Pam Harris, co-owner of Home Industry Bakery, noted the difference between her pepperoni rolls and the traditional Italian-bread rolls: "With a Home Industry pepperoni roll, you can bite into a soft bread—not have to rip it out of your mouth—and get the cheese in there that just makes the flavor. And we're known for that."

Home Industry Bakery has been around for nearly one hundred years in one form or another. It was originally named Home Trade Bakery, then Grace's Pastries, and now Home Industry Bakery—the name an homage to its Depression-era beginning when it operated as a consignment shop: home bakers would bring in products that the bakery would sell on their behalf. "Your grandmother would bake bread and bring in a couple extra loaves, and they would sell it for [her]," Mike Harris, Pam's husband and co-owner, explained. In the early 1930s, the company switched to baking its own products within the store.

The Clarksburg bakery has cycled through a few locations, first in the Adamston area, where a fire destroyed the building; then Main Street, where the landlord terminated the lease; and then downtown. The business has also

Left: Home Industry Bakery pepperoni roll lovers know which color bag to pick up at the local convenience store: red writing for pepperoni, purple writing for provolone cheese, or green writing for hot cheese.

seen four sets of owners in its long history, with the current couple, the Harrises, purchasing the bakery in 1984.

But Mike Harris had a relationship with the bakery long before then—a few of his uncles worked there when he was growing up, and at age twelve, he began working after school for two to three hours every evening washing dishes and sweeping the floor. Then, one payday when he was thirteen, nobody came to work. "They all went and got drunk," Mike recalled, "and I was there with [then owner] Bill McClain, and he said, 'I gotta make doughnuts and ain't nobody here to do it.'" Mike told McClain that he could do it. Having no other alternative, McClain took milk crates, turned them upside down, and built a kind of boardwalk for Mike so that he was tall enough to fry doughnuts. "He went from paying me like five

Left: Home Industry Bakery has been through a number of name changes since its opening some hundred years ago. Its current name reflects a time when people could sell their baked goods on a consignment basis at the shop. Today, Home Industry Bakery supplies pepperoni rolls to outlets all around West Virginia.

Above: Each Home Industry pepperoni roll has about twenty-three slices of pepperoni.

Above right: Home Industry Bakery initially made more baked goods and cakes, but as pepperoni rolls became more popular, more resources were devoted to them.

dollars a night as a kid to a hundred dollars a week. That made me the highest paid worker at Home Industry Bakery. At age thirteen."

At sixteen, Mike was able to work part-time and received more hours: four hours per evening after school and all day on Saturdays. Quickly, he began driving the delivery vehicle and shuffling pizza crusts and hoagie buns to local theaters and drive-ins. He took a seven-year hiatus to drive a city bus, but in the 1970s, the bakery called him back because it needed somebody to help out with the early morning shift from 3:30 a.m. to 10 a.m. "I was doing the work of three people, so he paid me three salaries," Mike said. When he finished his shift at the bakery, Mike would leave for his full-time job driving the bus.

Then, in the early 1980s, by which time he had become a professional cake decorator, Mike suffered a serious back injury. "They told me I would be paralyzed for life. So I was talking with Pam, and I was thinking, if I could just sit in a chair, I could teach people what to do and make sure stuff was done," Mike said. And as fate would have it, some personal events in then owner John Fragale's life resulted in him offering to sell the business to Mike and Pam. Pam was also already involved at the bakery, working part-time as a clerk.

In 1984, Mike and Pam had a daughter who was about five months old. "We were twenty-four years old and knew crap about business," Pam said. "I had only a high-school education—no college. We didn't know what we were doing." And they didn't have any money for Fragale's seventy-five-thousand-dollar asking price. But both of their parents put their houses up, and the Harrises were given a Small Business Administration (SBA) loan. "If it wasn't for the SBA," Pam said, "we wouldn't have been able to do it."

When the couple took over the bakery in the mid-eighties, they were producing about three or four dozen pepperoni rolls a day and just selling them out of the bakery's front door on Third Street in Clarksburg. Pepperoni rolls were secondary to the doughnuts, pastries, and cakes.

Today, pepperoni rolls are the primary seller; the couple had to ditch cakes in favor of more space to sort meat for the pepperoni rolls. Each Home Industry Bakery pepperoni roll has about twenty-three slices of Hormel pepperoni. And some have cheese.

"We started putting cheese on them when we'd eat them here, so we figured some customers might like them," Pam said. They were right; it was a particularly good seller among the high-school crowd that came in because of its similarity to pizza. They began adding cheese right into the roll with the pepperoni (always keeping some plain pepperoni, of course)—first provolone or mozzarella, and then hot-pepper cheese because they saw it was popular elsewhere.

The four-ounce rolls make up the majority of the bakery's business—about one thousand dozen a day. Twenty-three employees cover everything from baking, bagging, and delivery to working in the office.

"We have some people who have worked here for twenty and thirty years," Pam said. "We like to hire from within the community, and they really help make this work. It is not possible to do this without good people working for you."

Home Industry Bakery pepperoni rolls are sold primarily between Weston, WV, and Pittsburgh, going as far east as Cumberland, MD, and west

Below: The four-ounce pepperoni roll is the biggest seller, and the bakery makes about one thousand dozen per day.

to Parkersburg, WV. Rather than trying to steal customers from other local businesses, the couple purchased a vehicle and started doing deliveries, widening their circle of loyal patrons. Now, there are five or six drivers on the road daily stopping at thirty to forty GoMarts, thirty to forty BFS stores, Speedways, 7-Elevens, Par Mar stores, and Little General Stores.

"I like getting in the chain convenience stores because once you get in one, you can work your way into the other ones," Pam said. "And I like the mom-and-pop shops because they're the root of our country, and they try to keep the prices down and take care of their neighborhoods," Mike added.

And still, people come in from all over to purchase pepperoni rolls fresh from the bakery. Mike has even shipped to troops in Iraq. After a customer tried to ship rolls from two other bakeries that used preservatives, only for the rolls to end up

Below: Home Industry Bakery makes a number of pepperoni rolls—including a refrigerated one with peppers and cheese.

Below right: The mini pepperoni rolls, a favorite of co-owner Mike Harris, still use stick pepperoni.

moldy by the time they reached Iraq, Mike flash-froze his rolls and packed them in multiple layers of Styrofoam: success! "She called and told us they made it, and the troops loved it," Mike said.

Mike said that the old dough recipe and fresh ingredients help set their pepperoni roll apart.

"When I go to other states, they're like, 'What is this? A pizza roll?' and I'm like 'No! It's a pepperoni roll!'" Pam said. "Pizza, to me, has sauce, and there's no sauce in these. But I love talking to people about them. I think it's fun; if I could, I'd sell all day long."

Home Industry also sells a mini pepperoni roll, or "party pepps," which still contain stick pepperoni. They come a dozen to a bag, and as many as fifty are sold daily. The mini is Mike's favorite. "I eat one or two every day. I scramble an egg and put it in—got a sandwich for breakfast. I can throw some fried potatoes or something from the night before, and I got me a meat and potato sandwich. Anything goes good on them." Some of his customers take them home to eat with beans instead of bread or cornbread.

Home Industry Bakery also produces a larger roll with cheese and Oliverio Peppers. "We bake it, then we cut it and we add cheese and peppers inside. It has to be refrigerated," Pam said. "Nobody else does this. And we sell a lot."

Another specialty is a ramp pepperoni roll, made in limited quantities during the spring and sold only out of the store. "I put out a tray and it's gone within minutes," Mike said. "All we do is add ramps to it; pepperoni rolls go with anything."

And they're not done inventing. Mike is considering adding cheddar to the pepperoni roll lineup. The couple is also looking into creating an even larger pepperoni roll the size of half a loaf of bread, with twice the amount of meat as in their current large roll.

Ramps, a beloved Appalachian food, are a garlicky wild leek.

Ramps

REGIONAL FAVES

Left: The Donut Shop, a twenty-four-hour bakery located in Buckhannon, WV, produces about forty to fifty kinds of doughnuts every day, but the shop's pepperoni roll has drawn its own following.

19 N. LOCUST STREET
BUCKHANNON, WV 26201
304-472-9328

The Donut Shop

Traveling just a little bit farther south, you'll find the Donut Shop in Buckhannon, WV. Though it specializes in the named product, its pepperoni roll also has a following because it takes a different approach: "Our pepperoni rolls have crushed pepperoni," said manager Jimmy Anderson. "We grind it up, which I think is the appeal to it." Instead of folding sticks or slices into the dough, the shop adds a small mound of ground Hormel pepperoni into the center before baking, creating a pepperoni pocket from which the oils and spices of the meat can permeate the entire inside of the roll.

Garden & Gun magazine, a lifestyle magazine that covers Southern culture, featured the Donut Shop in its article "Rise & Dine: The South's Best Breakfast Joints." The piece noted that while pepperoni rolls may not be a typical breakfast, the ground pepperoni and dough combine for a piquant flavor unlike others found in this part of Appalachia.

Anderson, a Buckhannon native, said his first job was at the Donut Shop in 1997 or 1998. Twenty years later, much of the interior remains unchanged: a few booths line the windows, and regulars drink coffee at the two U-shaped counters. The orange and brown of the color scheme is left over from the building's first life as a Mister Donut. Through a large window that runs the

length of the side wall in the dining room, patrons can watch doughnuts being made. Customers on the go opt for the drive-through.

Until his passing in 2013, Richard Comegys, a Baltimore transplant who moved to West Virginia with a friend for the specific purpose of starting a doughnut shop, ran the business. Now, since ownership has transferred to Richard's brother Jack, who still lives in Maryland, Anderson is the man-on-the-ground, overseeing the day-to-day operations of the Buckhannon landmark, which produces forty to fifty kinds of doughnuts a day. Anderson estimates the shop adopted the pepperoni roll sometime in the 1980s, likely at the suggestion of a friend who had a recipe to contribute.

Typically, about half the Donut Shop's customers are regulars—both Buckhannon residents and West Virginia Wesleyan College students, Anderson said. Their busiest week of the year is during the West Virginia Strawberry Festival, held the third week of May. The workers are busy making strawberry-themed doughnuts because many Buckhannon natives who have moved away return for the festival and want a taste of home. When they're ready to leave town, they stop at the Donut Shop to pick up dozens of pepperoni rolls to take with them.

Currently, the Donut Shop does not offer shipping or wholesaling.

JR's Donut Castle

Perhaps taking a cue from the Donut Shop, JR's Donut Castle, a Parkersburg institution known for more than thirty-four types of doughnuts, has also added the savory pepperoni roll. The castle-shaped bakery makes five types: plain pepperoni, pepperoni with American cheese, pepperoni with pepper-jack cheese, pizza (pepperoni and pizza sauce), and pepperoni with jalapeño sauce.

JR's Donut Castle favors slices over sticks. Aaron Parsons, the manager who co-owns the business with his father and mother, JR and Darlene, claimed: "We cover more area with slices than sticks," adding that he never understood the appeal of the Slim Jim pepperoni.

Aaron is always looking to expand the menu, for the sake of innovation and also to meet customers' desires. "We just started the one that has jalapeños, because people were wanting a spicier one," he said. The new roll, which has to be refrigerated, contains pizza sauce mixed with jalapeños and, of course,

3318 EMERSON AVE.
PARKERSBURG, WV 26104
304-428-9097
JRSDONUTCASTLE.COM

Left: JR's Donut Castle, located in Parkersburg, WV, serves up more than thirty-four types of doughnuts.

pepperoni. The bakery's biggest sellers, though, are the rolls with cheese, but there's no clear winner between the American cheese and the hot-pepper-cheese rolls. "Every night they're neck and neck," Aaron said.

The Donut Castle, which opened in 1969 and operated only as a retail doughnut shop, was purchased by JR Parsons in 1977. He renamed the business JR's Donut Castle and expanded the shop's offerings to include a full-service bakery and cake shop. Aaron said the shop bakes every day, except for Saturday, with six bakers devoted to just pepperoni rolls. They sell eight-pack bags of two-ounce rolls to gas stations in the area, making about three thousand bags per night to meet demand. "Our wholesale is what keeps

Kara Moore   MEMORIES

"One time an older woman at our church who is a nonnative English speaker—she has spoken it for a long time and speaks it very well, don't get me wrong—was at an event where someone had brought pepperoni rolls. We were chatting and she casually asked if we had tried the 'salami rolls.' Both my husband and I sort of grimaced like that was the most disgusting thing we'd ever heard of. Then she corrected herself and said 'pepperoni rolls' and we were like, 'oh yeah, they're amazing, try one!' In reality salami and pepperoni are basically the same thing, but we were appalled at the idea of a salami roll. My husband, TW Moore, is from Rivesville in Marion County and has a very different idea of what a pepperoni roll is than I do. Basically: a pizza sub. (For me it's pepperoni, ideally a stick, baked into a yeast roll.) His grandmother worked for Colasessano's in Fairmont and brought them home often."

—Kara Moore, a native of Charleston, WV

us baking every single day. We sell a ton here, but we service so many gas stations and businesses with the pepperoni rolls," Aaron said. The bakery churns out twenty-five to fifty dozen in each flavor of the six-inch individually packaged roll each night as well.

The bakery prides itself in maintaining the integrity of its flagship products while also turning an eye toward innovation—for example, the recent addition of the jalapeño-sauce roll. During the last Super Bowl, the bakery started offering a two-foot-long pepperoni roll with thirty-five slices of pepperoni and six slices of cheese. Aaron said sales for that party-pleaser took off. On the sweet-meets-savory front, Aaron said they have also tried rolling up pepperoni in doughnut dough, "but that one would need a bit more testing."

Below left: Doughnuts are a big seller at JR's Donut Castle, but the American cheese and hot-pepper-cheese pepperoni rolls are also very popular. The shop bakes every day except for Saturday, with six bakers devoted to just pepperoni rolls.

Below: JR's Donut Castle serves five different kinds of rolls: plain pepperoni rolls, pepperoni rolls with American cheese, pepperoni rolls with pepper-jack cheese, pizza rolls with pepperoni and pizza sauce, and a jalapeño-sauce pepperoni roll.

THE SCIENCE OF MAKING A PEPPERONI ROLL

The Bread

Baking bread is an art. It's also a precise science that depends on the ingredients, when they're added, and in what proportion. Most basic bread recipes include four ingredients: flour, yeast, water, and salt. Josh Fernandez, a physicist and home baker originally from Charleston, WV, said that while mixing these ingredients may seem simple, the combination makes for a complex product. "Despite its requirement for precision, baking provides infinite variations when you switch out ingredients, add something else, bake at different temperatures and different humidities," Fernandez said. Even baking on different surfaces can affect the product.

For a pepperoni roll, the goal is a chewy, soft, flavorful bread. Thus bread flour is preferable to regular flour: its higher protein (gluten) content creates elasticity while at the same time giving the dough the necessary structure to hold its shape. Fat—butter, shortening, animal lard, or various oils—and salt contribute to softness and flavor. Yeast adds texture. Together these elements help control the protein structure—called gluten—that comes from mixing and kneading, Fernandez said. Some bakers use additional ingredients that contribute extra protein, like an egg or milk, which helps to control bubble formation.

Flour

First, the bakery adds yeast to water to wake the yeast up. Next, the bakery mixes its chosen bread flour with the yeast-water. The water enables gluten molecules to stretch out and form into long chains that create elasticity. Mixing and kneading (along with yeast) encourage those long chains, Fernandez said. The amount of kneading, however, affects the physical appearance and texture of the bread. More kneading results in a tougher, denser, and more uniform bread because air is pushed out and the gluten network in the dough becomes stronger the more it's worked. "Whether or not gluten formation is good or bad depends on the type of bread," Fernandez said. "But, for a pepperoni roll, we want some structure, and the softness will come about from other ingredients in the dough."

Below: Most basic bread recipes include four ingredients: flour, yeast, water, and salt.

Below right: Joel Brown, a Fairmont, WV, native, teaches a class on how to make pepperoni rolls.

Yeast

Bread's texture comes from fermentation, the activity of yeast. Yeast reacts with sugars in flour to create carbon dioxide, a process that creates the airy, bubbly texture and taste associated with bread. Yeast is often bought in three-pack packets from a grocery store. Maybe you use one right away, and leave the rest to languish in a cabinet or the fridge. But if you're serious about baking, you need to be serious about yeast too, according to baker Joel Brown, a Fairmont, WV, native who works at Rising Creek bakery in Mount Morris, PA. The bakery specializes in salt-rising bread, and Brown has offered a class on pepperoni rolls at this location. "The yeast is very important," said Joel, "and it's really important to make sure you're keeping it fresh and paying attention to it."

Yeast is first mixed with warm water to wake it up. Then, flour is added. Bakeries have the benefit of combining their ingredients with giant mixers. Colasessano's World Famous Pizza & Pepperoni Buns, for example, can mix up to 520 pounds of dough at a time, though they usually stick to about 225 pounds in a sixteen-minute spin.

As the flour is added and mixed in, the sugars within the flour disperse, making it easy for yeast to feed on the sugar. That creates carbon dioxide and alcohol. The amount of sugar in the flour (or added separately) will affect how much yeast is produced. Using a lot of yeast will affect the flavor and makes the dough "proof" quickly (not necessarily a good thing—according

Yeast helps bread to rise, but it also affects flavor. Using a lot of yeast makes the dough "proof" quickly, but bread—and pepperoni roll—dough that rises more slowly develops better flavors.

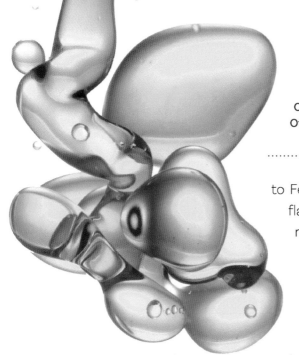

Oil is just one of a few "shorteners" that bakers use to make bread more tender. Other options used include butter or lard.

to Fernandez, bread dough that rises more slowly develops better flavors). Sugar, too, plays a role—primarily in flavor and holding moisture, as sugar attracts water molecules.

Fernandez said there are options once the yeast has activated and the dough is formed and covered. One way to proceed is to let your dough sit for about an hour at room temperature. "You'd be looking for the volume to double," he said. Then, after working the dough a little more, you'll be ready to bake. The other option is to put your dough in the refrigerator so it can proof overnight and develop more flavor. "Ultimately [it's] up to you when you're making these," Fernandez said. If you're baking at home, you might want to try it both ways to see if you notice a difference or have a preference.

After the yeast has done its job, it's time to add the fat or oil.

Fats and Oils

"We were having trouble one time," recalled John Menas, owner of Colasessano's World Famous Pizza & Pepperoni Buns. "Our dough was coming out like bricks." He had shown his employees how to mix the dough: always, water and yeast go into the bowl first, then the flour, and then the rest of the dry ingredients. The liquid has to saturate the flour *before* the oil is added. He cautioned that if you put oil on top of the dry flour, the flour will absorb the oil, blocking the path the water needs to begin gluten formation. "It all becomes bricks if [the flour] doesn't get hydrated with the water," Menas said. And that was the problem. Menas came in while they were mixing a batch of dough: "The girl grabbed that

Opposite, top: Butter, lard, or man-made fats like Crisco shorten the molecules in a pie crust and prevent the dough from becoming elastic.

Opposite, bottom: Pepperoni roll bakers use less shortening because they want their dough to be light and fluffy—but not flaky.

container with the right amount of oil and just poured it right on top of the flour. I about had a stroke—so we figured out that problem really quick."

Oil is just one of a few "shorteners" that bakers use to make bread more tender. Other options used include butter or lard.

For a delicious example of how shorteners work, Fernandez recommended getting a slice of pie—the crumbly, flaky crust is due to the use of butter (usually). "Structurally speaking, fat molecules are large, such that when mixed into doughs, they interrupt the gluten formation. More practically, oil covers bits of gluten to shorten the structure, hence their name as *shorteners*," Fernandez explained. The different fats and oils shorten the gluten structures in different ways, creating the different textures and structures of doughs and breads.

Once all the ingredients are added (including any secret ones!), individual rolls are prepared for baking. Dough is divided into balls—some bakeries do it by hand, weighing out a specific amount of dough or just eyeballing it, while other bakeries use a machine. Next the pepperoni (and sometimes cheese) is rolled up into the bun and transferred to the oven. Most bakeries have large ovens that rotate pans to ensure an even bake. After achieving the desired golden color, the pepperoni rolls are set to cool—or eaten immediately by a hungry, waiting patron (or home baker). Pepperoni is dry cured (uncooked) and closely related to salami.

The Pepperoni

While the science behind the bread is necessarily complex, the roll's crucial ingredient, pepperoni, is not as cut-and-dried as you would expect of a dry-cured (uncooked) meat.

Pepperoni comes as an edible casing filled with meat, salt, spices, and fat. The curing process, which encourages good bacterial growth, lengthens the shelf life of the meat, making it the perfect choice for workers over long shifts in the coal mines. Pepperoni is a type of salami (a type of cured sausage that originated in Italy), but pepperoni is often softer, smaller grained, and spicier, and usually made of inexpensive cuts of pork or beef, while salami might be made of virtually any meat.

Meat and Fat

Below: Spices such as black pepper, fennel, garlic, paprika, and cayenne pepper help give pepperoni its color and flavor.

The original creators of the pepperoni roll used pepperoni because it was cheap and available in a relatively poor area, Fernandez said. Cheaper meat, often from animals raised on corn and antibiotics, ends up having a higher

fat content because nonfiber carbohydrates, like those found in corn, cause a spike in insulin, which in turn causes fat accumulation. A sausage made with naturally lean meats needs added fat to keep it moist and flavorful. The naturally higher fat content of the pepperoni meats gives it its distinctive flavor and makes it satisfying as a meal.

And these fats and oils seep from the pepperoni into the bun during baking and attract many customers. Fernandez illustrated the importance of the grease: he had a friend in college who came to class every morning with a pepperoni roll for breakfast—which in itself isn't unusual. What struck Fernandez as odd is that his friend didn't eat the pepperoni. When Fernandez asked about it, his friend replied, "Oh, I don't care about the pepperoni, it's the oil that soaks into the bread that I want." "As the avid meat eater and West Virginia native that I am, this travesty bordered sacrilege," Fernandez said.

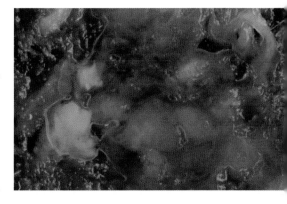

Above: For many customers, the fatty deposits in pepperoni are star of the show: the crucial element that makes the flavor distinctive and irresistible.

Salt and Curing

The grease is crucial not only for its moisture, but also for its flavors—salt in particular. Unbeknownst to most consumers of the pepperoni roll, salt does more than just flavor: it plays a pivotal role in the meat's dry-curing process by creating structure. "When salt is mixed in with meat and left alone overnight or so, salt will dissolve myosin [one of many kinds of proteins present inside muscle fibers, partly responsible for muscle contraction] where it collects around meat and glues meat together, creating the dense matrix that we expect out of pepperoni," Fernandez said. In addition, salt controls microbe growth and creates bacteria that feed off sugar to create acid, which gives the meat its tangy taste. It also lowers the pH, which is necessary for killing off the

harmful microbes. This curing process requires proper temperature and humidity to keep the pepperoni from spoiling.

Spices such as fennel, garlic, paprika, and cayenne pepper help give the pepperoni its color and flavor. Some of the color is also the result of added nitrates/nitrites, which are used in small amounts as a preservative in many cured meats.

The casings for cured and regular sausages were traditionally made from digestive tubes of animals, but modern appetites call for casings made from cellulose and/or collagen.

....

Spices such as fennel, garlic, paprika, and cayenne pepper help give pepperoni its color and flavor.

Pepperoni roll lovers tend to fall into two camps: those who favor stick pepperoni and those who favor sliced pepperoni. For a third, smaller contingent, ground pepperoni is the best.

John Menas, owner of Colasessano's World Famous Pizza and Pepperoni Buns, has just one word for slices: "Ehhhh."

STICKS!

Country Club Bakery and Tomaro's Bakery buy giant hunks of pepperoni that are cut by hand into sticks for pepperoni rolls. "I like everybody's pepperoni rolls, as long as they're using stick pepperoni," said Chris Palotta, owner of Country Club Bakery. He likes sticks because he believes they're better-quality pepperoni and put more meat into the bun.

Right: Traditional pepperoni rolls from the Italian bakeries tend to use stick pepperoni that is cut daily, like what is shown here from Country Club Bakery.

Opposite: Many bakeries opt for slices of pepperoni, like Rogers and Mazza's, whose owner said that people outside of the Clarksburg area prefer the slices.

Chris D'Annunzio, co-owner of D'Annunzio's Italian Bread, agrees that precut pepperoni is of a lesser quality than the stick pepperoni. "You get into different kinds of cheap pepperoni when you start getting it precut. I can't buy good pepperoni precut, not in the quality," D'Annunzio said. Changing the pepperoni in his rolls isn't an option, even if it's cheaper, because he doesn't want to disappoint his loyal customers: "People will come in this bakery and say it's too spicy or it's not good."

Colasessano's World Famous Pizza & Pepperoni Buns owner John Menas has just one word for slices: "Ehhhh." He also says it's a lot easier to put the appropriate number of sticks into a roll. "I don't know how many slices you would have to put in that pepperoni bun, but you would have to count the same amount each time for efficiency and consistency," he said. His bakers only have to count to five to get the right amount of sticks. "They can almost pick up what they need each time just from doing it so much."

Rogers and Mazza's (Marty's Bakery) owner Steve Rogers said that while the traditional stick pepperoni is popular in the Clarksburg area, people in other parts of the state appreciate slices. He also firmly believes that, as long as the product is Hormel, there is no difference in quality or taste. One reason Rogers goes with the sliced pepperoni is that it's more economical. Rogers's stepson and co-owner, Michael Mazza, said the sliced pepperoni has another benefit: grease. Many customers look for those orange-tinted pockets of spices and herbs, and with larger surface areas, slices deliver more grease.

Chico Bakery receives stick pepperoni—free of skin and bigger than regular slices—that is made specifically for the bakery and is then cut into slices. The

SLICES!

At JR's Donut Castle in Parkersburg, Aaron Parsons said his bakery uses only slices.

SLICES!

pepperoni hunks are deposited into a machine that slices it and drops it into place. "When steel touches the meat, the deterioration process begins," Chico Bakery supervisor Gary Miller said. "So when you buy a stick of pepperoni, you don't slice it until the day you use it." It's fresher that way, and it's always fresher than if you bought a bag of sliced pepperoni, he added.

Abruzzino's switched to the sliced pepperoni to be more cost-effective. The bakery also buys the presliced pepperoni because the slices come thinner than the bakery could produce, which makes them easy to spread throughout dough. The result? Pepperoni roll grease filtered throughout the bun.

At JR's Donut Castle in Parkersburg, Aaron Parsons said his bakery uses only slices—not just because of cost, but because it covers more area. "The slices seem to cover more of the roll," he said, "and people like that."

Home Industry Bakery's owners Mike and Pam Harris agreed that slices are the way to go—just a lot of them. They pack twenty-three slices into each pepperoni roll to make sure that each and every bite is meaty—the bakery's main goal. If Mike had it his way, though, he would have a different slice of pepperoni altogether: long pieces that were also wide. "I'd like to go back to that, but we mostly use the slices now because they're more economical," Mike said. He also finds it convenient that it comes presliced.

The Donut Shop in Buckhannon, one of the few bakeries in the state that makes pepperoni rolls with finely minced meat, asserts that its rolls contain more pepperoni throughout. "And it's less messy when you take a bite," said manager Jimmy Anderson.

All of the owners have their reasons. As the patron, though, it's up to personal preference (or where you were raised) which pepperoni camp you join.

"The slices seem to cover more of the roll," he said, "and people like that."

Sticks, slices, ground . . . it's up to personal preference (or where you were raised) which pepperoni camp you join.

GROUND!

The Donut Shop in Buckhannon, WV, is one of the few bakeries that serves crushed or ground pepperoni in its rolls.

PEPPERONI ROLLS

"SUPER DELICIOUS"

'700 EACH

A WEST VIRGINIA CONCOCTION

"yummy"

PEPPERONI SAUCE & CHEESE ROLLED IN SWEET D...

PEPPERONI ROLL PREVALENCE

While bakeries in North Central West Virginia planted the pepperoni roll seed, other businesses—and even schools—began to spread the product outside the area. Grocery stores, gas stations, and convenience stores around West Virginia often sell pepperoni rolls from local bakeries. Though not hot from the oven, they offer availability and ease while on the go. Schools make their own and serve them for lunch, or buy them from local bakeries to use as fundraisers. West Virginians clamor for them at sporting events; and even the military has brought them into rotation. Pepperoni rolls are everywhere.

School Lunches

Officials in the West Virginia Department of Education said several counties around the state, from the southern coalfields to the Northern Panhandle, serve pepperoni rolls as an entrée at lunchtime. It's not a surprise that it's often one of the favorite options.

Pepperoni rolls are so popular in Berkeley County that students request them, said Berkeley County Schools director of child nutrition and wellness Tracy Heck. "Popular is an understatement," echoed Chris

MEMORIES
Abigail Cioffi

"At Capital High School, pepperoni-roll day was the one day that almost everyone got school lunch. We could not wait to be seniors, because seniors got to go to lunch a few minutes early, which meant you could skip the inevitable line that formed to get lunch. They were giant and stuffed with pepperoni and cheese and made a great big greasy mess everywhere."

—Abigail Cioffi, a graduate of Capital High School in Charleston, WV

Derico, child-nutrition director for Lewis County Schools. "I usually menu them twice a month. If I did not, there would be a revolt." At Ritchie County Schools, pepperoni rolls are the school's biggest participation day—likely due to the smell of fresh-baked bread. There, the roll is always accompanied by the same sides: cottage cheese, pineapple slices, tossed salad, milk. When they have tried to change any of the items, the students were quick to let cooks know their disapproval.

In Grant County, however, students don't complain about variations in the menu. "Sometimes we use just the pepperoni, but sometimes we walk on the wild side and use cheese and marinara," child-nutrition director Tamera L. Gossard said. Similarly, Berkeley County's standard homemade roll includes

Tammie Toler MEMORIES

"I was never a huge fan of school lunches, but the day that cooks served pepperoni rolls in elementary and middle school might as well have been a holiday, because everyone ate school lunch on those days. The smell of the spicy pepperoni and the savory cheese blended with the warm, yeasty bread permeated the whole school, making all the students' mouths water and tummies growl throughout the building from 9:30 a.m. until whatever time lunch was served. My first experience with homemade pepperoni rolls came when my nanny discovered she could sell her homemade sourdough rolls alongside the homegrown goods she and Granddaddy raised on their 120-acre farm near Elgood. Eventually, curiosity got the best of her, and she added pepperoni and cheese to the homemade bread. They were delicious, although they wouldn't stay good indefinitely, they didn't have to be kept refrigerated to maintain a long shelf life."

—Tammie Toler, editor of the *Princeton Times* in Princeton, WV

the sliced pepperoni and melted mozzarella, but a marinara cup is available on the side. And Boone County cafeterias kick it up a notch by offering a side of banana peppers in addition to the mozzarella and marinara in their homemade pepperoni rolls, said Dee Krueger, child-nutrition director.

In addition to changing up the ingredients, some schools have tried to find ways to make the traditional roll a little healthier. Kanawha County Schools executive director of child nutrition Diane Miller makes her pepperoni rolls using a 51 percent whole-wheat dough and low-fat cheese. Fayette County child-nutrition director David Seay said they tried to use lower-fat turkey pepperoni, but the students responded that it was too spicy.

The number of pepperoni rolls sold varies from sixteen hundred each on pepperoni roll day in Grant and Ritchie Counties, to about four thousand in Logan County, forty-five hundred in Fayette County, twelve thousand in Berkeley County, and upwards of twenty-five thousand in Kanawha County. Most counties have been serving the rolls for more than twenty years, like in Marion County, even though they're a lot of work for the cooks because they're almost always made from scratch. "I actually have cooks who will call in sick on that day or take the day off," said Logan County Schools coordinator of child nutrition Anita Sedlock.

Fundraisers

Chris Pallotta, owner of Country Club Bakery, said that schools throughout the Fairmont area sell his pepperoni rolls at football games and basketball games as part of concessions that help fund

MEMORIES
Crystal Good

"Mrs. Eggleston was my elementary-school custodian and cook. She knew that my lunch favorites were kale, Salisbury steak, and pepperoni rolls. On pepperoni roll day, I didn't get two helpings like I did when she served me kale or the Salisbury steak, but I did get the biggest pepperoni roll! And that roll was made just for me with love in the school kitchen by hands that cared, that took the time to think about me. I thought about Mrs. Eggleston when I went to pick up my order of homemade rolls from the senior citizens at Rand Community Center. They make [them] for community organizations to use as fundraisers. They take preorders, you pay in advance, and pick up on a specific Saturday. I always freeze a bag for later. My favorite pepperoni rolls are made by hands that I know. The GoMart will keep you from being hungry, but pepperoni rolls made by hands that you know—feed your soul."

—Crystal Good, an artist, advocate, and entrepreneur from St. Albans, WV

MEMORIES

Whitney Humphrey

"When I was a kid, school parties weren't complete without homemade pepperoni rolls. I don't remember the first time I had one, but I've always loved them. Now that I have a family of my own, I make pepperoni rolls from time to time as a treat for my family (and me). There's just something about the warm bread and gooey cheese and the heat from the pepperoni that all come together so deliciously. It's so hard to eat just one!"

—Whitney Humphrey,
a Charleston, WV, native and editorial writer
at the *Charleston Gazette-Mail*

area schools. Rogers and Mazza's Italian Bakery provides special discounts for pepperoni roll fundraisers within its delivery area, from homeless missions and the Salvation Army to food pantries, churches, and schools.

Gas Stations

People often cite pepperoni rolls as falling into one of three categories: homemade, from the bakery, or from the gas station. While the best pepperoni rolls are often the hot, fluffy, and fresh kind straight from an oven, don't dismiss the third category: the gas-station pepperoni roll. Many bakeries, such as Rogers and Mazza's Italian Bakery and Home Industry Bakery, supply gas stations with prepackaged rolls that can be found on shelves or in the refrigerated section. They are a quick option in a convenient place—perfect for both residents and visitors.

Military

According to the West Virginia Humanities Council's *West Virginia Encyclopedia*, pepperoni rolls have even permeated the US military. A version is included in military MREs (meals ready to eat). Although they're produced by a North Carolina company, West Virginia natives can get a taste of home while serving their country.

Left: The SHOP 'n SAVE in Morgantown, WV, makes pepperoni rolls in-house.

MEMORIES *Molly McClain Cribbs*

"We would try to get out early of the class we had before lunch so we could be first in line in case they sold out of pepperoni rolls [from DeFelice] for fundraisers. Or we'd beg the teacher, 'It's only two minutes early! We need pepperoni rolls!'"

—Molly McClain Cribbs, a Follansbee, WV, native

MEMORIES

Brannan Lahoda

"They are ubiquitous. Holiday parties, family reunions, tailgates. Pepperoni roll days were always circled on the monthly school lunch calendar. As a kid, my mom would bake them the night before WVU football and basketball games, and we would eat them on the drive to Morgantown. Whenever I go back to West Virginia, I know I'm home when I bite into a pepperoni roll and wash it down with a beer or 'shine. And I rarely leave the state without taking a bag for the road. I love them."

—Brannan Lahoda,
a St. Albans, WV, native

Ballparks, Arenas, and Stadiums

While others may opt for hot dogs, popcorn, or peanuts at sporting events, West Virginians often choose a pepperoni roll.

West Virginia University Coliseum and Mountaineer Field at Milan Puskar Stadium

West Virginia University's Milan Puskar Stadium (football) and Coliseum (basketball/multisport complex) serve Julia's Pepperoni Rolls from Chico Bakery, regular or with provolone, and heated in the original packaging. But many fans make their own instead for tailgating: small, bite-sized rolls to large, sliced-up versions can be found on trays on the back of trucks, on tables, and in hands in parking lots across Morgantown on game days.

Appalachian Power Park

The West Virginia Power, a minor-league baseball team of the South Atlantic League and the Class A affiliate of the Pittsburgh Pirates, plays at Appalachian Power Park where, in 2013, the then director of food and beverage, Nate Michel, announced a new signature menu item: a two-pound pepperoni roll called the "vandy roll." While the massive roll—priced at sixteen dollars and intended to feed multiple people—was only around for one season, it did make it to the 2013 Minor League food fight challenge.

The MiLb.com food fight competition pits minor-league baseball's monstrous, delicious, creative concessions against one another in a

social-media-driven contest that consists of four different categories: gut busters, hogs 'n' dogs, local legends, and scrumptious sandwiches. Sadly, the vandy roll, which competed in the local legends category, ultimately lost out to the Lakewood BlueClaws' Clawd's Crab Cake.

Monongalia County Ballpark

The Monongalia County Ballpark is home to the West Virginia University baseball team and the West Virginia Black Bears minor-league baseball team, which began playing in the New York-Penn League in 2015 as an affiliate of the Pittsburgh Pirates. The stadium offers a variety of ballpark concessions—and of course its take on the classic pepperoni roll. After slicing it down the middle, the Julia's Pepperoni Roll from Chico Bakery can be "loaded" with the Custard Stand's chili and drizzled with nacho cheese for a solid ballpark meal that requires two hands.

Above: The Monongalia County Ballpark offers a Julia's Pepperoni Roll from Chico Bakery, which can be "loaded" with the Custard Stand's chili and drizzled with nacho cheese.

The West Virginia Black Bears host an event similar to the famous Pittsburgh Pirates, who celebrate the Eastern European heritage of their host city with a great Pittsburgh Pierogi Race N'at, in which people clad in pierogi-shaped costumes race around the baseball stadium between innings. During every Black Bears baseball game, Chico Bakery sponsors a pepperoni roll character race around the field to honor West Virginia's Italian immigrant influence via pepperoni roll costumes. "We had three costumes made for the three varieties of pepperoni rolls," Gary Miller, Chico Bakery supervisor said: Hot Pepper Hank, Double Stuffed Dave, and Pepperoni and Cheese Patty.

Right: The West Virginia Black Bears host a pepperoni roll race between Hot Pepper Hank, Double Stuffed Dave, and Pepperoni and Cheese Patty.

"When you see their faces, you get a better idea of each individual personality," said John Pogorzelski, assistant general manager of the Black Bears. "We have our female character; and we have our evil, mischievous guy; and we have our character who has trouble winning races." Pogorzelski, originally from Buffalo, NY, knew pepperoni rolls had to have a place at the baseball games—both as something to eat and as someone to cheer for—as soon as he tried his first one. Although the arrogant Hot Pepper Hank and Pepperoni and Cheese Patty split most of the wins, Double Stuffed Dave comes out as the lovable underdog. All of the characters have fun with it, and so do the fans. "People get the pepperoni roll race," Pogorzelski said, "they like it, they cheer it on, and people get into it."

Pogorzelski also thinks the pepperoni race is a great thing for Morgantown and West Virginia because it symbolizes everything the Black Bears are about—healthy, family fun in a friendly atmosphere—and it gives the locals something to call their own: "There's no pepperoni roll race that has taken place in California or Nebraska or New York."

THE PEPPERONI ROLL MAKES MEDIA HEADLINES

The humble pepperoni roll, created for the depths of coal mines, has made on impression on media—from large, national media publications to small, quarterly ones. The largest and most notable publication to document the pepperoni roll's rise to fame is the *New York Times*. In the September 2009 article "Fast Food Even Before Fast Food," John T. Edge wrote of local bakeries, convenience stores, and restaurants serving up the coal miner's meal as a "vestige of the state's bituminous coal mining industry" and Italian immigrant heritage.

In an April 2013 article in *Bon Appetit*, "West Virginia's Iconic Pepperoni Roll Is Finally Getting Some Official Recognition," Josh Dean talks of the legislation to make the pepperoni roll the official state food. The Morgantown High School graduate noted the classifications of pepperoni rolls:

Like its spiritual cousin the pizza slice, a pepperoni roll varies greatly in taste and quality, and the taxonomy ranges from flour-dusted, brownie-size rolls stuffed with sliced pepperoni and sold by the dozen in bread bags at gas stations; to individually wrapped rolls as big as an overstuffed burrito with pepperoni sticks in the middle, sold at Mountaineer Field, home of West Virginia University's football team; to heated rolls, split open and topped with cheese and tomato sauce, such as those served at Colasessano's in Fairmont. Sticks versus slices is probably the biggest divider among bakers—sticks is definitively the purist's take, and what Country Club uses—but you'll also find some hackles raised over the matter of cheese. (I'm fairly agnostic on the issue, but if you opt for cheese, go with pepper jack, which adds a kick that complements rather than overwhelms the spicy meat).

Gourmet Magazine published "Alto Appalachia" by Jane and Michael Stern in January 2007. The article highlights Tomaro's, Country Club Bakery, S&B Bakery and Cafe (now closed), DiCarlo's Famous Pizza, and others:

A sheaf of pencil-thin twigs of pepperoni is folded inside a tube of yeast dough. After the dough has risen, the whole thing is baked: that's a pepperoni roll, the savory snack of choice throughout north-central West Virginia. A cooked roll is a wieldy handful about 4 inches long and resembles the border of a thick pizza. Inside, the red sticks of spicy sausage occupy a tight tunnel, the bottom of which has been moistened by their hot-oil seepage. The sides and top remain soft and fluffy.

Andrew Zimmern, from Travel Channel's *Bizarre Foods with Andrew Zimmern*, visited with a local in 2012, learned about the history of the pepperoni roll, and tried his hand at baking a few.

Pepperoni rolls also made an appearance on *Roker on the Road*, a Food Network show featuring *TODAY* show weatherman and cohost Al Roker, who traveled across the country to find good eats.

Goldenseal, the magazine of West Virginia traditional life, featured the pepperoni roll on its cover in the spring 2006, volume 32, number 1 issue. "The

Pepperoni Roll: State Food of West Virginia" by Colleen Anderson followed the history of the pepperoni roll and its prominence.

WV Living magazine has an annual "Best of West Virginia" award that allows readers to vote for their favorite eateries, entertainment venues, celebrities, and more. One category was devoted to the best pepperoni roll. In 2013, Colasessano's took home the honor, and in 2014 it went to Country Club Bakery.

These prominent mentions of the pepperoni roll are just a portion of the media coverage it has received in recent years. Countless articles and videos have been produced, not only on the history but also on the debate over which bakery dishes out the best ones, and publicity is likely to continue as word spreads beyond West Virginia's borders.

Right: The pepperoni roll made the cover of *Goldenseal*, a magazine that celebrates West Virginia, in 2006

PEPPERONI ROLL CRUSADES

West Virginians answer the call when the pepperoni roll is threatened, whether in a friendly contest or by corporate decisions. Supporters of the regional treat stand in solidarity to assert the roll's place at the table.

2013 CQ Roll Call Taste of America

In 2013, CQ Roll Call, a media company specializing in congressional news, hosted its third annual CQ Roll Call Taste of America, sponsored by the National Beer Wholesalers Association, the National Restaurant Association, the National Pork Producers Council, and the American Frozen Food Institute. The contest is an online March Madness tournament-style food competition that pits regional foods from around the country against one another. Each state has a minimum of one entry, with additional entries for larger states, and brackets are divided into geographic regions. Beating out sixty-four other foods, including finalists such as Arizona's chimichangas, Georgia's peach cobbler, South Carolina's shrimp and grits, Maryland's crab cakes, Oregon's pear tart, and even Iowa's bacon, West Virginia's pepperoni roll emerged with the votes to take the title.

Beth Bronder, senior vice president and publisher of CQ Roll Call, said a record number of votes were cast: "The Elite Eight dishes that made it to the

MEMORIES

Chad W. Cottrill

"I drove two and half hours from Pittsburgh to Bridgeport to get fresh pepperoni rolls one Sunday afternoon after church last week—they were so good!"

—Chad W. Cottrill,
a Bridgeport, WV, native

finals clearly have a proud following, but the West Virginia pepperoni roll fans really went the extra mile, taking to social media in order to win the top prize."

A trophy was presented to Sen. Joe Manchin and other members of the delegation at a "Taste of West Virginia" event on behalf of the state of West Virginia. "I am thrilled to hear that our state's beloved and humble pepperoni roll has been recognized for its deliciousness and rich flavor," Manchin said in a press release. Country Club Bakery, Colasessano's World Famous Pizza & Pepperoni Buns, and Julia's Pepperoni Rolls from Chico Bakery were all in attendance.

You Can't Outsource the Pepperoni Roll

Sheetz, a gas-station/convenience-store chain headquartered in Altoona, Pennsylvania, with more than 437 locations in Pennsylvania, Maryland, Virginia, West Virginia, Ohio, and North Carolina, announced in July 2015 that it intended to stop carrying West Virginia–produced pepperoni rolls. The social media outcry was palpable.

At the time, Sheetz carried three West Virginia-made pepperoni rolls: Rogers and Mazza's Italian Bakery, Home Industry, and Abruzzino's Italian Bakery.

Steve Rogers, owner of Rogers and Mazza's Italian Bakery, said he was blindsided when Sheetz told him the convenience store was no longer going to carry his pepperoni rolls. Instead of the locally made rolls, he said, Sheetz was opting for an out-of-state provider. For Rogers, that

The Great Sheetz Controversy of 2015: Facebook® Feedback

meant losing distribution to 117 Sheetz stores across three states—a fourth of his company's business—and possibly necessitating laying off some of his thirty-three employees.

Rogers and Mazza's urged customers via Facebook to voice displeasure, and the post was shared more than 2,500 times, with hundreds of likes. Before long, local media ran the story, and hundreds upon hundreds of people took to Sheetz's Facebook page to comment on any post and leave reviews.

Sheetz's public-relations manager Tarah Arnold released a written statement, citing the reason for the change as part of Sheetz's ongoing effort to ensure quality and consistency in its pepperoni roll offerings:

Currently, we have four vendor partners providing pepperoni rolls to our stores. Three of those vendor partners are West Virginia-based companies. To ensure consistency throughout the company, we have identified the need for one vendor to supply this product, and that evaluation is ongoing. We appreciate our customers' passion around our offerings and thank them for their feedback during this evaluation process.

Arnold went on to acknowledge the significant role West Virginia has played in the growth of the company and to reiterate Sheetz's commitment to the communities it serves in the state through employment, the selection of Morgantown as the flagship market for the new Sheetz store concept, and donations to local food banks, which totaled more than one hundred thousand dollars in 2014. At that time in 2015 Sheetz had fifty-two store locations in West Virginia that

"No more Rogers and Mazza's Pepperoni Rolls? Guess I'll be finding another place to stop. . . . That was one of the big reasons I went to Sheetz! Those pepperoni rolls are the best!"

"Put back the West Virginia Pepperoni Rolls in all Sheetz."

"You need to use local products! Very disappointed and I'll think before pulling into a Sheetz next time. Hope you will correct your mistake."

"The pepperoni roll was invented in WV. What makes you think you can expand so much in our state and yet outsource a WV staple and we will be ok with it. I'm boycotting and sharing with my friends too!"

employed more than fourteen hundred West Virginians, with plans to open more locations.

Customer feedback on Facebook also prompted company executives to hold a meeting with the bakery owners at Sheetz's main distribution center in Claysburg, PA. Shortly afterward, Sheetz reversed its decision to stop carrying West Virginia-made pepperoni rolls in West Virginia stores. However, the company's desire for consistency led Sheetz to choose one West Virginia bakery supplier for its in-state stores rather than all three of the previous vendors. To make the announcement, Sheetz also took to Facebook:

> We want our customers to know that we listen to their feedback and truly take their opinions into consideration. Our goal is to ensure that pepperoni rolls made in West Virginia are in every Sheetz location in West Virginia. We are currently evaluating many potential West Virginia-based partners to fulfill this need. These new partnerships will allow for a more consistent offer and ultimately a better customer experience. We thank our West Virginia customers for their honest feedback and their support during this evaluation process.

A few months after the crisis began, Sheetz selected Home Industry Bakery as its exclusive pepperoni roll provider to all of its West Virginia stores. Home Industry had already supplied pepperoni rolls to about fifteen Sheetz stores in Maryland and Pennsylvania and twenty stores in West Virginia. All West Virginia Sheetz locations began carrying Home Industry pepperoni rolls on September 12, 2015.

And while Rogers and Mazza's Italian Bakery was not ultimately selected to provide pepperoni rolls for Sheetz, co-owner Dennis Mazza noted that the bakery has since expanded into Circle K stores and Pittsburgh-area 7-Elevens.

PEPPERONI ROLL EVENTS

Pride in the West Virginia–heritage food also takes the form of cook-offs, contests, fairs, and festivals that pop up each summer. From small, local baking contests to large competitions, the answers to who can make the best pepperoni roll—or who can eat the most—are often discovered at the bottom of an empty paper bag.

Golden Horseshoe Great Pepperoni Roll Cook-Off

While R. J. Nestor and David Scoville were writing the musical *Golden Horseshoe*, a celebration of West Virginia's history and heritage, they were also brainstorming ideas for fundraising events. "My wife, Elisha, suggested a pepperoni roll cook-off because they are so specific to the region," said Nestor, who, along with Scoville and the Morgantown Theatre Company, organized the event.

On August 25, 2013, at the Wesley United Methodist Church in downtown Morgantown, nearby restaurants, including Anthony's Pizza, Terra Cafe, Gracious Grains, the Bakery, the Cupcakerie, and Rising Creek Bakery, competed to see who could concoct the best pepperoni roll in two divisions: traditional and gourmet. Three judges tasted their way to a verdict, crowning Gracious Grains the winner of the traditional division, while Terra Cafe, which continues to sell its rounded rolls in its restaurant, won the gourmet division.

Nestor has since held an additional bake-off in 2016 and intends to host others in the future.

The Golden Horseshoe: A Musical for West Virginia

Nestor and Scoville created the *Golden Horseshoe* musical in honor of West Virginia's 150th anniversary of statehood. The musical showcases a father reconnecting with his West Virginia heritage as he teaches his eighth-grade son about the state's history in preparation for his Golden Horseshoe Test. Each year West Virginia's eighth-grade students test their knowledge of the state's history, geography, economy, and government. The highest scorers on the test receive a pin to commemorate their achievements. The program takes its name from golden horseshoes given to fifty early explorers who, in 1716, under the organization of Alexander Spotswood, governor of the Virginia colony, went west of the Allegheny Mountains—where West Virginia now sits. The governor presented each with a small golden horseshoe in honor of their bravery during the mission.

West Virginia Three Rivers Festival

WVTHREERIVERSFESTIVAL.ORG

The West Virginia Three Rivers Festival—an arts and culture festival that celebrates Fairmont—has morphed over the years. It began as a two-day event called Septemberfest. It became the corporate-sponsored Three Rivers Coal Festival, which celebrated Marion County's strong coal history and honored Fairmont's three rivers: the Monongahela, the Tygart Valley, and the West Fork. As coal mining declined, the name and focus changed again; Three Rivers Festival and Regatta moved locations to the riverfront and rescheduled for warmer weather. After a brief adjustment in 1997 to highlight local history, in 1998 it finally became the West Virginia Three Rivers Festival and took on a new focus: the pepperoni roll. Since Fairmont is the most commonly credited birthplace of the pepperoni roll, C'Anna Keffer, a member of the festival's board of directors and the festival's teen queen in 2002 and queen in 2007, said it's only natural

Above: The West Virginia Three Rivers Festival is an arts and culture festival that celebrates Fairmont—the most commonly credited birthplace of the pepperoni roll. The festival has started to largely focus on the pepperoni roll in recent years.

that the city celebrate its culinary heritage. The logo even features an Italian-bread pepperoni roll with several pieces of stick pepperoni poking out.

In 2010, the festival began incorporating pepperoni roll events, including a pepperoni roll toss for kids; a professional pepperoni roll bake-off; and an eating contest, now properly named the West Virginia Three Rivers Festival Pepperoni Roll Eating World Championship. The only bigger mouthful is during the contest. While the roll toss didn't make it past the first year, the other events became mainstays.

The sixth-annual professional pepperoni roll bake-off was held in May 2015. To honor the winner of the bake-off, the festival commissioned a trophy in the figure of a coal miner carrying a lunch bucket. Mining company Consol Energy

Guy Ward MEMORIES

"While I was growing up, I ate a lot of pepperoni rolls, not knowing that someday they would play a major role in my life. It's once a year that the pepperoni roll becomes this big part of my life during the West Virginia Three Rivers Festival. It's during this festival that we hold the biggest eating event in West Virginia and one of the biggest in the country at Palatine Park in downtown Fairmont. It's called the Pepperoni Roll Eating World Championship and professional eaters from all over the country come to it. I'm the main person who puts this event together each year. I'm responsible with making the arrangements with the International Federation of Competitive Eating aka Major League Eating, and for setting up the interviews between the news media and the contestants. Every year we draw some of the highest-ranked eaters in the world. . . . The hope is that someday it will be as big as the Nathan's Famous Hot Dog Eating Contest that's held every year on July 4 at Coney Island."

—Guy Ward, mayor of White Hall, WV

sponsored the trophy, which travels with the winning bakery each year. Home Industry Bakery won the competition in 2010 and 2011, but since then the trophy has been changing hands. In 2012, Papa Bears (now shuttered) won, followed by Noteworthy Sweets in 2013, and Country Club Bakery in 2014. In 2015, it was the Firehouse Cafe in Fairmont, and in 2016 it was Vito's Pizza from Clarksburg.

The year the festival's pepperoni roll eating contest debuted, it was an amateur event. The competition pitted West Virginia University's basketball team against the Fairmont State University team. WVU player Joe Mazzulla won, downing six rolls in five minutes. It was impressive, at the time. But by the next year, the event went pro.

The popularity of the event attracted a sponsoring organization, Major League Eating, which now brings in professionals, such as Joey "Jaws" Chestnut—the man who once stuffed down seventy hot dogs and buns in ten minutes at the Nathan's International Hot Dog Eating Contest—to compete in the festival's Pepperoni Roll Eating World Championship. The first professional

Opposite: To honor the winner of the West Virginia Three Rivers Festival Pepperoni Roll Bake-Off, the festival commissioned a trophy that features a coal miner carrying a lunch bucket, the delivery method for many pepperoni rolls that make their way into the earth as part of a coal-miner's lunch.

Below left: In 2010, the festival hosted its first ever bake-off between professional restaurants in the area.

Below: The pepperoni roll bake-off receives more than a dozen entrants who show off their best rolls for a panel of judges.

competition, which bumped the time up from five to ten minutes, was held in 2011, and the winner blew Mazzulla's record out of the water: Pat "Deep Dish" Bertoletti, ranked number two at the time, ate 30.5 pepperoni rolls to set the first world record. The next year, Bertoletti broke his own record by eating thirty-three rolls—that's more than six pounds of pepperoni rolls in ten minutes.

Bertoletti's record stood for the next two years: in 2013, Joey Chestnut won with twenty-eight, and in 2014, Matt "Megatoad" Stonie won with thirty-one. But in 2015, things changed: Stonie broke his own personal record, as well as the world record, by eating thirty-four pepperoni rolls in ten minutes and winning the $8,750 in prize money. Number-four-ranked Miki Sudo came in second place with 28.5

Right: The West Virginia Three Rivers Festival hosts a Pepperoni Roll Eating World Championship each year where the world's best eaters compete. Matt Stonie holds the world record for the number of pepperoni rolls eaten. Stonie, a San Jose, CA, native, had never tried a pepperoni roll until he competed in the 2014 pepperoni roll eating contest.

rolls, and number-seven-ranked Adrian "The Rabbit" Morgan placed third with twenty-three. In 2016, Geoffrey Esper, the number-ten competitive eater in the world, won the competition by eating twenty-three pepperoni rolls in ten minutes.

The then 130-pound, twenty-three-year-old Stonie was ranked as the number-one eater worldwide. He's put down 182 strips of bacon in five minutes, 14.5 pounds of birthday cake in eight minutes and twenty pounds of pumpkin pie in eight minutes. The San Jose, CA, native was thrilled to win the pepperoni roll–eating contest his first year: "Even though I won the competition," he said, "I really wanted a record. So it's great to come back and finally beat it." Stonie said his strategy is to start off as fast as possible because he knows he begins

Below: In 2014, Matt "Megatoad" Stonie (center) ate thirty-one pepperoni rolls in the pepperoni roll eating competition; and in 2015, Stonie broke his own personal record, as well as the world record, by eating thirty-four pepperoni rolls in ten minutes. In the 2015 pepperoni roll eating competition, number-four-ranked Miki Sudo (left) came in second place with 28.5 pepperoni rolls, and number-seven-ranked Adrian "The Rabbit" Morgan (right) placed third with twenty-three pepperoni rolls.

to slow down toward the end. "You just have to make as much space for all the bread as you can," he said.

Because the pepperoni roll is a regional delicacy, competitive eaters have a difficult time building a strategy around a food they have never or seldom tried, but they rely on their skills in the three main components of competitive eating: jaw strength, stomach capacity, and hand-speed coordination. George Shea, chairman of Major League Eating, said pepperoni rolls are similar to hot dogs in that jaw strength is important with dense dough, as is stomach capacity. Hand-speed coordination is more important in competitions like chicken wings, where eaters have to maneuver quickly and easily to take the meat off the bone.

Right: The winner of the pepperoni roll-eating competition receives a belt. Image Credit: Guy Ward.

Stonie said the pepperoni roll is also similar to the hot dogs in that you can dunk them. Many contestants opted for water or Kool-Aid to help soften the rolls quickly because there's not enough time to produce the necessary quantities of saliva.

Country Club Bakery is the competition's only official pepperoni roll supplier. They make about fifty-five dozen fresh, uniform rolls for the event. Guy Ward, mayor of nearby White Hall and West Virginia delegate, has been involved with the festival for about eight years and explained the decision: "We chose Country Club Bakery because they've been making pepperoni rolls since 1927, and not much has changed in the way they bake them. Because of this, they're very consistent in size and weight, and in an eating contest, we realize that's very important." He said the average-sized Country Club roll weighs about 3.25 ounces, with the pepperoni making up almost a third of the weight. The average size is about 5.5 inches long by 2.5 inches wide by two inches thick. Inside each are three sticks of pepperoni, sliced in a long, square shape that measures about 4.5 inches long by 5/16 of an inch wide by 5/16 of an inch thick.

Above right and right: Pepperoni rolls can be found at fairs and festivals around the state, including the Autumn Harvest Festival in Pocahontas County. Homemade pepperoni rolls are often found at vendor booths and include personal touches—like spicy cheeses or added bacon.

Other Fairs and Festivals

Pepperoni rolls can be found at nearly every festival across the state of West Virginia, even if they are not a main focus. Here are some of the most popular ones:

Mountain State Art & Craft Fair

MSACF.COM

Since 1963, the Mountain State Art & Craft Fair held in Ripley has celebrated high-quality craftsmanship in West Virginia, featuring artisans, crafts, demonstrations, competitions, music, events, and local foods.

In 2015, in its first year participating, the American Culinary Federation's West Virginia chapter produced various baked breads and rolls to sell, including a garlic pepperoni roll. The group sold one thousand rolls or more each day of the fair and could have sold nearly twice that if they had been able to make them, according to Bob Milam, current vice president and former president of the chapter. "We couldn't make them fast enough for the people who wanted them. We just didn't have enough people," he said. "Next year, though, we are going to do better."

The pepperoni rolls, originally anticipated to be a side item, were one of the biggest sellers the group produced, right behind cinnamon-raisin bread. Milam said the recipe for the coveted pepperoni roll at the fair is simple and is similar to a traditional roll, but with the addition of brushed butter, sprinkled garlic, and Romano-cheese seasoning, a spice blend from one of his suppliers. "We were taking them out of the oven and putting them right in bags to hand to customers," he said. Many customers bought one or two dozen to take home.

Below: The American Culinary Federation's West Virginia chapter produced a garlic pepperoni roll to sell at the Mountain State Art & Craft Fair in Ripley, WV.

Monongalia County Fair

MONCOUNTYFAIR.ORG

Amid the fried Twinkies, Philly cheesesteak sandwiches, and corn dogs at the Monongalia County Fair, the vendors selling the homemade pepperoni rolls always have lines reaching out far past the food trucks.

A handwritten sign pointing customers in the right direction doesn't need much elaboration: "Homemade pepperoni rolls with chili or cheese." Patrons, hungry between rides, concerts, motorsports events, and the car show, are happy to wait.

West Virginia Italian Heritage Festival

WVIHF.ORG

The annual West Virginia Italian Heritage Festival, held in Clarksburg since 1979, is a three-day event that draws more than one hundred thousand visitors. Vendors sell *fritti* (an Italian deep-fried doughnut ring), organizers run an annual pasta cook-off, and, of course, there are pepperoni rolls. D'Annunzio's Italian Bakery sold its stick pepperoni rolls, and the Bluebird, known locally for its fried chicken, also served up hot pepperoni rolls.

Top right: Pepperoni rolls at fairs and festivals often come loaded with a homemade chili and hot cheese sauce, like the one seen here at the Monongalia County Fair.

Above right: The West Virginia Italian Heritage Festival began in 1979.

Right: D'Annunzio's Italian Bakery sold its pepperoni rolls at the West Virginia Italian Heritage Festival.

Upper Ohio Valley Italian Heritage Festival

ITALYFEST.COM

The Upper Ohio Valley Italian Heritage Festival, held in Wheeling in July, is another celebration of Italian food, including the pepperoni roll.

Mountain State Forest Festival

FORESTFESTIVAL.COM

The Mountain State Forest Festival, one of the largest and oldest festivals in the state, is held each October in Elkins, WV. Vendors from across the area bring their homemade pepperoni rolls to sell—which fly off the tables so quickly, more often need to be made to accomodate the next day's demand.

Feast of the Seven Fishes Festival

MARIONCVB.COM/EVENT/FEAST-SEVEN-FISHES

Another popular Fairmont festival is the Feast of the Seven Fishes, held on the second Saturday in December to celebrate the Italian Christmas Eve tradition. The festival was born when Marion County native Robert Tinnell, a writer and filmmaker, wrote a graphic novel in 2005 based on his family's experience of celebrating the feast. The large Italian population in the area took hold of the Catholic tradition that celebrates the sacraments as family gathers for the meal. The two-day festival features a cooking school (often featuring fish entrées); live entertainment; shopping; and food vendors, some of whom, of course, sling pepperoni rolls (without fish).

MEMORIES *Leisha Elliott*

"I really don't remember not knowing about pepperoni rolls. During my school years, you could always tell the days when pepperoni rolls were on the menu in the cafeteria, because the line would be extra long. And it was hard to concentrate right before lunch because you could smell them baking throughout the school. There is nothing better than stopping by Country Club Bakery as a fresh batch of pepperoni rolls comes out of the oven. You are hard-pressed not to eat one (or two) when you get in the car. Colasessano's takes the pepperoni roll to a whole new level. Their version is more of a pepperoni bun. In my opinion it is best eaten with cheese, [meat] sauce, and peppers that have been cooked in a special tomato sauce. This is the same meat sauce that we also eat on our hot dogs. It's funny, when you grow up with pepperoni rolls, you assume everyone knows what they are. I think people in West Virginia—especially in North Central West Virginia—take them for granted. It has just been in recent years that I realize that is not the case. We have been using pepperoni rolls more and more to brand the state and Marion County. People identify with food, especially food from certain regions, and for us, pepperoni rolls are that food. The history of the pepperoni roll also makes for a great story about the early years in North Central West Virginia, which is one of the reasons we often brand ourselves as 'Italy in Appalachia.' With a single food, we are able to explain our early history."

—Leisha Elliott, executive director of the Marion County Convention and Visitors Bureau

Notable West Virginians offer their GUT REACTIONS

Edited selection from the *Charleston Daily Mail*'s (now the *Charleston Gazette-Mail*) April 22, 2013, article, "Notable West Virginians Offer Their Gut Reactions," wherein famous West Virginians opine on the pepperoni roll's status as the official state food:

■ Newsweek/Daily Beast special correspondent and editor of "Democracy: A Journal of Ideas" Michael Tomasky holds a special place in his heart for the pepperoni roll.

TOMASKY
Newsweek
correspondent

"I'm Italian on my mom's side, so I grew up gobbling down my maternal grandmother's pepperoni rolls by the dozen. I was shocked when I moved away from the state and saw that they didn't exist everywhere," Tomasky said.

"I've since introduced pepperoni rolls to many friends and never had one person say anything other than 'Wow, these are great!' And now, of course, more and more people have discovered them. So I'm all for it. They're the state's greatest export since Jerry West."

Michael Tomasky's Vote: Pepperoni Rolls

■ Former governor and current **Sen. Joe Manchin** echoed Tomasky's sentiment.

"Our beautiful state is so special because we have a great variety of foods and traditions," Manchin said. "Of course, I am very partial to pepperoni rolls and spaghetti and meatballs because these are foods that I grew up with, but I also appreciate and enjoy many other great foods from our state such as hot dogs, pinto beans and cornbread, ramps and apple butter. Indeed, West Virginia has something for everyone to enjoy."

Joe Manchin's Vote: Pepperoni Rolls

■ **Chuck Yeager**, the first pilot to travel faster than sound, can think of a better choice.

YEAGER
Legendary
test pilot

"Never heard of pepperoni rolls. Who is making this decision? Only ever had cornbread & buttermilk & leather britches," he said.

For those who don't know, leather britches are beans that are strung together and then hung up to dry. They are then boiled, usually with a ham bone and onion for added flavor.

■ **Sen. Jay Rockefeller**, who helped protect pepperoni roll bakeries from stricter USDA regulations that may have put them out of business in 1987, stands by the pepperoni roll's side. He has even given pepperoni rolls away as Secret Santa gifts to other senators.

"West Virginia has no shortage of culinary treasures — from apple butter and buckwheat cakes, to mealtime staples like beans and cornbread," Rockefeller said. "And I've been to more ramp dinners than I can count. What's great about the pepperoni roll is it is a uniquely West Virginia creation. For that reason, it holds a special place in our hearts. And I'm glad I could play a part in keeping it around."

Jay Rockefeller's Vote: Pepperoni Rolls

■ **Jessica Lynch**, former U.S. Army soldier who served in Iraq during the 2003 invasion, was making pepperoni rolls at the time of the interview.

"We are a big fan of pepperoni rolls in my house. My daughter loves them. My fiance goes nuts for them. I like to make them," Lynch said. "I think it's a

LYNCH
Former Iraq
prisoner of war

cool little back story that they were invented here in West Virginia in Fairmont. I think that's neat."

"I guess my only concern is that we have such a high obesity rate. But I'm definitely a fan of pepperoni rolls."

As far as beans and cornbread? "I'm not a fan, only because that's what we ate all the time was beans and cornbread growing up. It's the poor man's food," she said. "I understand where pepperoni rolls are coming from to be the official food."

Jessica Lynch's Vote: Pepperoni Rolls

Aviation legend says he has never heard of pepperoni rolls

■ **Secretary of State Natalie Tennant** said, "I will support the pepperoni roll being the state food for many reasons. First off, it originated in West Virginia. It was the ingenuity of a West Virginian — a coal miner. I think that exemplifies what West Virginia is all about."

Tennant, who is from Marion County — home of the pepperoni roll, promotes it whenever she has the chance, including at conferences and visits.

"The thing for me is, you can look to various bakeries and find a pepperoni roll. Tomaro's Bakery and Country Club Bakery might dispute who was first. And in Fairmont, there's a different kind of pepperoni roll — it's Colasessano's, they call theirs a pepperoni bun. They are all awesome."

"I have always promoted all things West Virginia — West Virginia grown, made, created. I think that the pepperoni roll is a great example of that. It's not that I don't promote others. What about ramps? I love ramps. Beans and cornbread — those are all awesome meals that people will want to promote. But the pepperoni roll — people just love them. It makes me proud to say they came from my home county."

Natalie Tennant's Vote: Pepperoni Rolls

■ The Charleston Daily Mail's own Food Guy, **Steven Keith**, has waxed poetic about pepperoni rolls in his columns over the years.

"As a 'serious food dude,' I should probably be horrified by the prospect of glorifying something as simple as a pepperoni roll. But if done right, man, are they good!" he said.

"And I'm not talking about the ones you get at the local shop-a-minute, but really good ones — fresh-baked and still oven-warm from a bakery in Clarksburg or Fairmont. I know it's not gourmet food, but it's a soul-satisfying snack with a noble history behind it. West Virginia could do a lot worse when it comes to celebrating a state food. Ramps are good also-ran but, hey, they only show up a few months a year. We need a state food that can commit to full-time indulgence!"

Daily Mail Food Guy's Vote: Pepperoni Rolls

PEPPERONI ROLLS

■ "Naming Pepperoni Rolls as the West Virginia state food wasn't about a popularity contest. A better question is, what other popular food items were BORN in West Virginia"
— **Todd, Poca**

■ "Pepperoni rolls are the best West Virginia food because it was created here in West Virginia, at first for our coal miners"
— **Lola, Lenore**

"*I've been to more ramp dinners than I can count. What's great about the pepperoni roll is it is a uniquely West Virginia creation. For that reason, it holds a special place in our hearts. And I'm glad I could play a part in keeping it around.*"

—US Senator Jay Rockefeller

Natalie Tennant

MEMORIES

"I thought, growing up in Marion County the youngest of seven, that my mom created the pepperoni roll. . . . We would cut the pepperoni; it would be so hard to cut into sticks from a big long log. . . . We never bought them. When you have seven kids, you can't go buy a dozen here or there. We couldn't afford it. . . . But now, pepperoni rolls are an essential part of my life because when I began in the office, I wanted to have a reception and have pepperoni rolls to show my heritage. Tomaro's makes the mini pepperoni rolls, so we bought many dozens of the mini pepperoni rolls, and it became my signature reception fare. It's a staple of mine. If you want a whole meal, you might get Colasessano's with everything on it, or for a quick snack you can have in your purse or to take fishing, then you might go with Country Club. And D'Annunzio's is located in the little neighborhood in Clarksburg [North View] where my mother grew up and where she got bread for her family. . . . There's Rogers and Mazza's, Chico's . . . it's really part of what makes our state so unique and so diverse. . . . The pepperoni roll is so versatile. My daughter got into theater, and the parents were waiting on theater practice to be over, and we knew these kids hadn't eaten. I jumped up and went to Kroger and got a couple dozen pepperoni rolls. They can be a quick snack, I've eaten them for breakfast before, they can be a meal, a delicacy. That's why they're one of the greatest foods ever invented—especially because they're from West Virginia. . . . I think it's a definition of who we are, with how it got started—ingenuity and perseverance—people will say 'what are those?' and we push them and say 'here, just try it,' and they love it. Then they ask why they don't have them in their state!"

—Natalie Tennant, former West Virginia secretary of state

SO GOOD IT SHOULD BE ILLEGAL

The pepperoni roll has seen its fair share of legislation—whether through trying to enact stricter food-handling processes or through trying to elevate the pepperoni roll to become the official state food.

Bakery Classifications

The future of pepperoni rolls was threatened in 1987 when the USDA sought to reclassify West Virginia's small bakeries that produce pepperoni rolls as meat processors. US Senator Jay Rockefeller fought the motion, however, which would have required stricter safety and sanitation requirements. Rockefeller argued that the USDA certified pepperoni before it came to the bakeries, requiring that the meat was already preserved through curing, fermentation, and drying.

The reclassification could have resulted in more than one hundred thousand dollars in costs to the small bakeries for the installation of concrete floors with drains. Rockefeller said that such expenses would have delivered a devastating blow to the pepperoni roll. He contacted the then secretary of agriculture Richard Lyng to discuss the decision. The USDA decided to hold bakeries that produce pepperoni rolls accountable only to the existing inspection standards, ensuring they survived.

Legality in Other States

Steve Rogers of Rogers and Mazza's said their bakery ran into trouble shipping their pepperoni rolls across state borders. Some states, he said, refused to allow products on the shelves that contained meat completely enclosed inside of dough. "It had to be visible for whatever reason, or it had to be refrigerated. And ours sits on the shelf," Rogers said. "Virginia was one. Jay Rockefeller helped us out and grandfathered us into some clause to make it legal. I remember spending hours on the phone back in the 1990s."

Jimmy Anderson, manager of the Donut Shop, said they experienced the same troubles: "The thing of it is, with a lot of states, they don't allow you to sell them. They consider pepperoni a meat, so they don't allow you to keep it on the shelf."

But is this pushback across state borders law or legend?

Lisa Ramsey, southwest regional manager for the Virginia Department of Agriculture and Consumer Services Food Safety Program, said if there were ever a law against pepperoni rolls being sold on shelves in Virginia, it is no longer the case. "Pepperoni rolls are not illegal in Virginia," she said. "I have no idea why that may be a rumor."

Ramsey noted that Virginia, too, went through a scenario in which pizza shops or food establishments had to adhere to stricter restrictions if meat were served. For example, if only vegetables were served on a pizza, it would not need additional regulation, but if sausage or pepperoni were added, it would. Ramsey said that pepperoni was granted an exemption.

Official State Food

In 2013, the West Virginia legislature sought to name the pepperoni roll the official state food. Unfortunately, the resolution was referred to the House Rules Committee to be placed on the calendar for a vote, where it remained until the end of the session without any further action. However, the resolution is still worth a read, if for nothing other than the state pride it inspires.

Delegate Joshua Nelson, R-Boone, sponsored House Concurrent Resolution No. 84. Whether or not it is legally recognized, the pepperoni roll is West Virginia's state food in every native's heart, mind, mouth, and stomach.

HOUSE CONCURRENT RESOLUTION NO. 84
(By Delegates J. Nelson, R. Smith, Caputo, Tomblin, Iaquinta, Miley, Marcum, White, Moore, Manchin and Andes)
Declaring the "pepperoni roll" to be the official State Food of West Virginia.
Whereas, Often referred to as the "unofficial state food of West Virginia," the simple-to-make pepperoni roll is more than the sum of its parts, every single bite is filled with soft, warm bread infused with flavor from the freshly cut, delicately seasoned pepperoni;

MEMORIES
Courtney Balestier

"My strongest memories of pepperoni rolls are of the ones my grandmother used to make, not actually in West Virginia but in Appalachian Pennsylvania (Uniontown). Still, my favorite pepperoni rolls are the ones most like hers: made with stick pepperoni, not sliced, with a good, low bread-to-pepperoni ratio. (I'm not crazy about cheesy pepperoni rolls, which seem to me to defeat their original intention as low-maintenance packed lunches.) My grandmother would keep them in the same large square Tupperware container where she would keep bread buns, made with the same dough. The container lived on top of the dryer, in the room off the kitchen that we called 'the porch' even though it was indoors, and that was the first place anyone would go upon entering her house. I make them now, but anyone who's ever tried to make a family recipe knows something intangible is lost in translation. Mine are good, but they'll never be as satisfying."

—Courtney Balestier, a journalist and self-proclaimed pepperoni roll connoisseur

" . . . eaten cold or hot, this simple food continues to sustain West Virginians from every walk of life. . . ."

and

Whereas, Philadelphia may have its cheese steak and New York its bagels, the pepperoni roll was first created in Fairmont, around 1927 by Italian immigrant baker, Giuseppe "Joseph" Argiro, and it should be no surprise that it quickly became a daily staple for coal miners and struggling families;

and

Whereas, In 1987 when the United States Department of Agriculture proposed restrictions that threatened to put the family-owned bakeries of pepperoni rolls out of business, West Virginia Pepperoni Roll producers contacted Senator Jay Rockefeller who intervened and successfully saved the entire industry;

and

Whereas, Today, the humble pepperoni roll is ubiquitous around the mountain state and may be found in restaurants, bakeries, convenience stores and family kitchens, eaten cold or hot, this simple food continues to sustain West Virginians from every walk of life, coal miners, artists, business people and students;

and

Whereas, Country Club, Tomaro's and Chico's Dairy are only a few names that may not be in business today if the proposed change had been implemented. The pepperoni roll is as popular as ever and is enjoyed everyday throughout West Virginia and the states that our bakeries supply; therefore,

be it
Resolved by the Legislature of West Virginia:
That the Legislature hereby recognizes the significance of the "pepperoni roll" in the state and by so doing declares that the "pepperoni roll" is the official State Food of West Virginia; and,

be it
Further Resolved, That all citizens of West Virginia to join in recognizing the value and importance of pepperoni rolls in West Virginia; and,

be it
Further Resolved, That the Clerk of the House of Delegates, forward certified copies of this resolution to the pepperoni roll bakeries of West Virginia (House Concurrent Resolution 84, 2013).

Below: West Virginia's State Capitol at night. Image courtesy of Nagel Photography / Shutterstock, Inc.

PEPPERONI ROLLS AROUND THE STATE

Keeping with Tradition

The historic bakeries in North Central West Virginia may have started the pepperoni roll phenomenon, but as the cuisine caught on, many restaurants across the state have stepped up to help popularize and carry on the tradition as part of their regular menus or as daily specials. Here are a few worth noting:

North Central West Virginia

Fairmont area

Noteworthy Sweets

Noteworthy Sweets makes an award-winning roll split and filled with cheese and marinara.

9I FAIRMONT AVE., FAIRMONT, WV 26554

304-366-6683

HTTPS://WWW.FACEBOOK.COM/NOTEWORTHY-SWEETS-I6433I250245572/

8th Street Confectionery

8th Street Confectionery offers it plain, with sauce and cheese, or with peppers.

301 EIGHTH ST., FAIRMONT, WV 26554

304-363-9503

HTTPS://WWW.FACEBOOK.COM/8TH-STREET-CONFECTIONERY-266147926264/

Clarksburg area

Ritzy Lunch

Ritzy Lunch pepperoni rolls can come with chili, cheese, or peppers.

456 W. PIKE ST., CLARKSBURG, WV 26301

304-622-3600

Bridgeport area

Della's Deli

Della's Deli serves regular and minis.

230 E. MAIN ST., BRIDGEPORT, WV 26330

304-842-2902

HTTPS://WWW.FACEBOOK.COM/DELLAS-DELI-LLC-836095946419462/

Nutter Fort area

Bonnie Belle's Pastries

Bonnie Belle's Pastries is known for its party trays.

1520 BUCKHANNON PIKE, CLARKSBURG, WV 26301

304-622-7471

HTTP://BONNIEBELLESPASTRIES.COM/SITE

MEMORIES

Kacie Kidd

"There was a little Italian restaurant in the next town over from where I grew up. They made pepperoni rolls with so much grease they would soak through half a dozen napkins. They were the most delicious things I've ever eaten. I cried when that restaurant burned down."

—Kacie Kidd, a Wellsburg, WV, native

Central West Virginia

Buckhannon

Brakes Dairy King

Brakes Dairy King offers homemade pepperoni rolls as part of its daily specials on Thursdays. Rolls are ready by 7:00 a.m.

2 CLARKSBURG RD., BUCKHANNON, WV 26201

304-472-2337

HTTP://WWW.BRAKESDAIRYKING.COM/

Mid-Ohio Valley

Parkersburg

The Pizza Place

The Pizza Place has a cult following for its tasty pizza, but its pepperoni rolls are not to be dismissed. They have two locations:

SOUTHSIDE—1410 BLIZZARD DR., PARKERSBURG, WV 26101

304-485-7327

DUDLEY AVENUE—2208 DUDLEY AVE., PARKERSBURG, WV 26101

304-485-5601

HTTP://WWW.THEPIZZAPLACE.ORG

Northern Panhandle

Weirton

Barney's Bakery

Barney's Bakery is a purveyor of rolls of all kinds: nut rolls, apricot rolls, poppy-seed rolls, and, of course, pepperoni rolls.

460 PARK DR., WEIRTON, WV 26062

304-748-4370

HTTPS://WWW.FACEBOOK.COM/BARNEYS-BAKERY-1435004046825282/

New Martinsville

Pasco's Pizza

Pasco's Pizza makes a mean pizza in addition to its famous pepperoni rolls.

660 THIRD ST., NEW MARTINSVILLE, WV 26155

304-455-4555

Eastern Panhandle

Shepherdstown

Shepherdstown Sweet Shop Bakery

Shepherdstown Sweet Shop Bakery dishes out a pepperoni-cheddar roll that has locals raving.

100 W. GERMAN ST., SHEPHERDSTOWN, WV 25443

304-876-2432

HTTP://WVBAKERY.COM

Metro Valley

Charleston

Starlings Coffee & Provisions

Starlings Coffee & Provisions offers meat and vegetarian versions.
1599 WASHINGTON ST. E., CHARLESTON, WV 25311
304-205-5920
HTTP://STARLINGSWV.COM

Barboursville

Big Loafer

Big Loafer—sounds like bread, but you'll find pepperoni rolls there too.
404 HUNTINGTON MALL #660, BARBOURSVILLE, WV 25504
304-733-0424
HTTPS://WWW.FACEBOOK.COM/THEBIGLOAFER

New River/Greenbrier Valley

Gap Mills

Kitchen Creek Bakery

Kitchen Creek Bakery makes fresh pepperoni rolls and homemade bread.

5510 SWEET SPRINGS VALLEY, GAP MILLS, WV 24941

304-772-4253

HTTPS://WWW.FACEBOOK.COM/KITCHEN-CREEK-BAKERY-I467755258669940/

Beckley

Calacino's Pizzeria

Calacino's Pizzeria stuffs pepperoni and mozzarella inside house-made dough, bakes it to perfection, and serves it with a side of marinara.

3611 ROBERT C. BYRD DR., BECKLEY, WV 25801

304-253-1010

HTTP://WWW.CALACINOS.COM

Lewisburg

The Bakery

The Bakery makes fresh batches of pepperoni rolls daily.

102 N. COURT ST., LEWISBURG, WV 24901

304-645-1106

HTTP://WWW.THEBAKERYLLCWV.COM

Around the State

Gino's Pizza & Spaghetti House

Gino's Pizza & Spaghetti House is a West Virginia pizza and pasta restaurant chain serving freshly made pepperoni rolls at its various locations.
GINOSPIZZA.COM

The Modern Pepperoni Roll

Everyone loves a traditional pepperoni roll, and that won't change. But for something familiar with a twist, restaurants have begun taking modern approaches to the classic, creating "gourmet" pepperoni rolls that include other meats, vegetables, or even a change in appearance.

Richwood Grill

Chef Marion Ohlinger, who helped pioneer the farm-to-table movement in Morgantown, owned the now-defunct Richwood Grill. The restaurant hosted a Global Feature Dinner Series that featured about a dozen themed dinners throughout the year, and in 2013, Ohlinger hosted the Fifth Annual Appalachian Deconstruction & Gastronomy Dinner. In addition to buckwheat-battered frog legs, ramps, and pawpaw ponzu, Chef Ohlinger presented a pepperoni roll cupcake. "It was the traditional flavor in a new presentation," Ohlinger said. The pepperoni roll was baked in a cupcake wrapper and topped with mozzarella "icing" and a cherry tomato. Ohlinger has since continued his creations at a new restaurant, Hill & Hollow.

Opposite: Former Morgantown restaurant Richwood Grill created a pepperoni roll cupcake, complete with a mozzarella icing and a cherry tomato. Image Credit: Eric Clutter/ Richwood Grill.

Above: Atomic Grill also sells pepperoni, cheddar, and pickled-pepper pepperoni rolls.

Atomic Grill

Atomic Grill, a punk rock BBQ restaurant in Morgantown, is known for its diverse, welcoming environment. It has also become known for social activism—through its menu items.

The first instance came in 2014 in response to an online comment that waitresses should "show some more skin." So they did: potato skins. In an event that made national news, the restaurant served potato skins and donated 100 percent of the proceeds to the West Virginia Foundation for Rape Information and Services.

A year later, Atomic Grill once again expressed its support through food. When the state legislature considered a bill in 2015 that could have threatened the civil rights of the lesbian, gay, bisexual, and transgender community, the owners took a stance through pepperoni rolls.

The Atomic crew, led by then co-owner and West Virginian Dan McCawley, who remembered fondly his after-school snacks of pepperoni rolls, combined two of their favorite things about West Virginia: the diversity of people and the pepperoni rolls. They sold two pepperoni rolls that pushed the envelope—one with pulled pork, cheddar, and pepperoni and the other with pepperoni, cheddar, and pickled peppers. Five of the seven dollars charged for each plate went to Fairness West Virginia, an organization that advocates for the equal rights and fair treatment for all lesbian, gay, bisexual, and transgender West Virginians. More than four hundred rolls were sold.

Atomic Grill
595 GREENBAG RD., MORGANTOWN, WV 26501
304-241-1170
WWW.FACEBOOK.COM/ATOMICGRILL

Schmitt's Saloon

Country music, cowboy boots, and fried foods prevail at Schmitt's Saloon in Morgantown. The pepperoni rolls are no exception to the over-the-top theme: they are stuffed with pepper-jack cheese, deep fried, and served with homemade marinara.

Schmitt's Saloon
245 CHEAT RD., MORGANTOWN, WV 26508
304-291-9001
WWW.SCHMITTSSALOON.COM

Apothecary Ale House & Cafe

Beer is king at Apothecary in Morgantown, which boasts one of the most comprehensive lists of brews in town. While its food offerings are limited to a few paninis and appetizers, there's also a pepperoni roll from Chico Bakery with the option of cheese, grilled on the panini press and served with a side of marinara.

Apothecary Ale House & Cafe
227 CHESTNUT ST., MORGANTOWN, WV 26505
304-291-2291
HTTPS://WWW.FACEBOOK.COM/APOTHECARYALEHOUSECAFE

Above: Atomic Grill, located in Morgantown, WV, sold two modern pepperoni rolls to raise money for Fairness West Virginia. This pulled-pork pepperoni roll featured melty cheddar.

Above: The Terra Cafe pepperoni roll is a simple combination of quality pepperoni, egg wash, Parmesan, and herbs, but it also comes as a vegetarian-friendly option. Image Credit: Sher Yip.

Terra Cafe

Known for fresh food, innovative vegetarian and vegan meals, and locally sourced products, Terra Cafe also produces a classic pepperoni roll with Parmesan, herbs, and a crispy crust that has won accolades.

Terra Cafe
425 INDUSTRIAL AVE., MORGANTOWN, WV 26501
304-554-2133
HTTP://WWW.TERRACAFEWV.COM

Jeff's Breads

Jeff's Breads, located about twenty minutes north of Lewisburg in Renick, specializes in European-style breads baked daily using a starter said to be over four hundred years old. In addition to the artisan breads, Jeff's produces a pepperoni roll full of sliced pepperoni baked in a fluffy dough. The secret to this delicious roll? Jeff said it's the real butter.

Jeff's Breads
304-497-2768
HTTP://WWW.JEFFSBREADS.COM/

DiCarlo's Original Pizza

The story of DiCarlo's Pizza in the Ohio Valley goes back more than one hundred years, beginning with a grocery store, then a bakery business, and finally its famous square pizza. Today, most DiCarlo's locations serve pepperoni rolls as part of its limited menu, with the exception of the Steubenville, OH, and the Wellsburg, WV, locations.

DiCarlo's Original Pizza
HTTP://WWW.DICARLOSPIZZA.COM

Morgantown Brewing Company

Microbrewery Morgantown Brewing Company reopened in 2009, revitalizing West Virginia's oldest operating brewery. In addition to on-site craft brews, it also offers food that often incorporates its own beer. One small plate is a twist on the traditional: grain rolls stuffed with pepperoni, capicola, and salami and served with *queso blanco* and marinara.

Morgantown Brewing Company
1291 UNIVERSITY AVE., MORGANTOWN, WV 26505
304-292-6959
HTTP://WWW.MORGANTOWNBREWING.COM

The Cupcakerie

Morgantown's first and only cupcake bakery churns out tasty sweet treats, like Red Carpet Red Velvet, P'Nutty for Chocolate, and Gold and Blue-berry. But the shop also makes a savory snack: its traditional-tasting pepperoni roll looks a little different: shaped as a cupcake and wrapped in cupcake paper.

The Cupcakerie
194 WILLEY ST., MORGANTOWN, WV 26505
304-212-5464
HTTP://THECUPCAKERIE.COM

Mid Atlantic Market

The Mid Atlantic Market, located in the Pierpont Landing plaza in Morgantown, is a small, upscale marketplace specializing in items delivered fresh from the Strip District in nearby Pittsburgh, particularly Italian grocery items, deli foods, cheeses, salads, olives, and roasted coffee. It also sells homemade pepperoni rolls individually, in five-pack mini sizes, or as party trays. In its version, sliced pepperoni is wrapped around the center, providing mouthfuls of meat each time.

Mid Atlantic Market
7000 MID-ATLANTIC RD., MORGANTOWN, WV 26508
304-777-4686
HTTP://WWW.MIDATLANTICMARKET.COM

Meagher's Irish Pub

Featuring traditional Irish fare, New Celtic cuisine, and Irish ale, Meagher's Irish Pub is not the traditional eatery where one would find a pepperoni roll. However, the pub has perfected its own nontraditional recipe: ground pepperoni rolled in an airy dough, shaped like a doughnut, deep fried, and served with creamy ranch dressing.

Meagher's Irish Pub
26 BETTEN CT., SUITE 101, BRIDGEPORT, WV 26330
304-848-9200
HTTP://WWW.MEAGHERSIRISHPUB.COM

Green Arch Market

Located in the Greenmont neighborhood of Morgantown, Green Arch puts a special spin on the pepperoni roll, combining it with a college town favorite: pizza.

Green Arch Market
260 GREEN ST., MORGANTOWN, WV 26501
304-381-4918
HTTPS://WWW.FACEBOOK.COM/GREENARCHMARKET

Rolling Pepperoni

Pepperoni roll enthusiasts are more than willing to travel for their favorite roll, but now the roll is on a roll, or, more accurately, on wheels. Katherine Schuler's Rolling Pepperoni, a Pittsburgh-based food truck, takes the pepperoni roll to music and arts festivals and more.

Rolling Pepperoni
HTTP://WWW.ROLLINGPEPPERONI.COM

Above: Meagher's Irish Pub, located in Bridgeport, WV, serves a deep-fried, doughnut-shaped pepperoni roll with a side of ranch.

Adaptations for Dietary Concerns

The pepperoni roll is pretty straightforward in its main ingredients: bread, pepperoni, sometimes cheese. But dietary restrictions and food allergies can make one or more of these ingredients a problem, so some bakeries are adapting to spread the beloved treat to all.

Venerable Bean Bakery

The Morgantown-based vegan baking company operates from Mountain People's Co-Op and offers sweet treats like mini cakes, cookies, muffins, and pies, as well as bagels, soups, and pepperoni rolls. Its vegan version of the pepperoni roll uses a soy/wheat gluten-based "pepperoni" with an organic bread.

Venerable Bean Bakery
137 PLEASANT ST., MORGANTOWN, WV 26505
HTTP://WWW.VENERABLEBEAN.COM

Terra Cafe

This Morgantown cafe serves a vegetarian-friendly roll with feta cheese, sundried tomatoes, and spinach in addition to its parmesan and herb pepperoni roll.

Terra Cafe
425 INDUSTRIAL AVE., MORGANTOWN, WV 26505
304-554-2133
HTTP://WWW.TERRACAFEWV.COM

Starlings Coffee & Provisions

Located in Charleston and specializing in organic, small-batch pastries, sandwiches, soups, and stromboli, Starlings offers meat and vegetarian versions of the pepperoni roll.

Starlings Coffee & Provisions
1599 WASHINGTON ST. E., CHARLESTON, WV 25311
304-205-5920
HTTP://WWW.STARLINGSWV.COM

Recipes

THE GREAT PEPPERONI ROLL EXPANSION

The pepperoni roll is so uniquely West Virginian that it's difficult to find outside of the state's borders. If you find yourself far from the region of the roll but craving the nostalgic comfort and taste of home it provides, try out one of these recipes created by expatriates. They're not exactly the traditional rolls, but you might discover a new favorite (or at least a decent substitute until you can visit again).

Daniel Oliver

MEMORIES

"My grandfather, Antonio Silletta, at age twenty-two emigrated from San Giovanni in Fiore, Calabria, Italy, in 1923 to Watson in Marion County, West Virginia. He was unmarried at the time. Soon he got a job as a hand loader [pick and shovel] at the Watson Coal Mine. He had a brother and sister living there at the time. Their family name got Americanized to "Slate" and there are still Slates in Watson. In 1925, he moved to Star City and married my grandmother.... Pepperoni is not an Italian salumi (yes, that is the correct spelling). It is not native to Italy and cannot be found there. Rather, it is an Italian-American creation. It was always a staple when I was growing up. My grandparents had several sticks in the refrigerator at all times. My grandmother, known for years as Lizzie Slate (later it got changed back to Silletta though) was Star City's best bread baker, hands down. Each week of her life, she baked bread using a twenty-pound bag of Robin Hood-brand flour. That is a huge amount of dough. Her mixing bowl was a fifty-gallon wine barrel, cut in half. She often stuffed pepperoni into some of that wonderful dough and made small pepperoni rolls for her coal-miner husband and their five children. My grandmother's recipe didn't get written down. That is not unusual. We watched her work and later we tried to imitate her bread baking as best we could over the years, and the recipe [Watson Coal Mine Pepperoni Rolls] is our adaptation."

—Daniel Oliver, a Morgantown, WV, native, lawyer, and avid Italian baker/chef

Watson Coal Mine Pepperoni Rolls

- 8 cups bread flour
- ½ cup whole wheat flour
- ½ cup sugar, plus ½ teaspoon
- 2 tablespoons active dry yeast
- 4 teaspoons salt
- 4 cups warm water
- ½ cup olive oil
- 8 cups of thickly sliced Margherita-brand pepperoni

In large stand mixer bowl, add flour, ½ cup sugar and salt. Turn on speed one or two to thoroughly mix. In a large cup, take 2 cups of the warm (approximately 100 degrees) water and add the yeast and ½ teaspoon sugar. Whisk with a fork and let stand for five minutes (proof). Should have about a ¼-inch head on it, like a beer. In a separate cup, combine ¼ cup olive oil with the remaining 2 cups water. Turn mixer on speed two, and drizzle in the yeast mixture. Then, drizzle in the water/olive oil mixture. Let it knead on speed two for approximately 7 minutes. Remove dough from bowl, and place in a plastic container or bowl with enough room for it to double in size. (Tip: Put dough in a clear container. Place a rubber band around the outside, at the level of the dough, making it easy to see when size has doubled.) Cover container with a lid or clean kitchen towel. Let dough rise in a draft-free area. Once dough has risen, take it out of the container, and place on a lightly floured surface. Working one at a time, cut off approximately 3 ounces of dough from the ball. Roll it out to about a 6-inch circle. Toward the edge of the circle, place about 4 slices of pepperoni

MEMORIES

Bethany Knowles Hall

"How happy am I that my mom volunteered in elementary school and was given the ever-coveted recipe from our fifth grade teacher. Challah-bread pepperoni rolls equal heaven! Too bad I never mastered the recipe; glad I have a friend that did though!"

—Bethany Knowles Hall,
a South Charleston, WV, native and
executive director of the Alzheimer's
Association, West Virginia chapter

on the dough, overlapping each piece. Begin to roll the dough over, jelly-roll fashion; then place 2 to 3 more pieces of pepperoni in the middle of the circle. Continue to roll the dough jelly-roll style, and seal/crimp the edges closed. Place rolls on a baking sheet, cover with a towel, and let rise for 1 hour. Bake at 350 degrees for 40 minutes, or until light golden brown. Brush tops of rolls lightly with the beautifully flavored pepperoni oil left on the baking pan after removing from oven.

NUMBER OF SERVINGS: 25
PREPARATION TIME: 1 HOUR

Personal Notes from Daniel Oliver: You could also add mozzarella, Monterey jack, or pepper jack cheese to the filling, and/or some roasted peppers. Pepperoni rolls are also delicious served like this: split the baked roll in half length-wise, fill with some pasta sauce and mozzarella, close up, and toast in the oven until crusty. The coal miners at Fairmont Coal Company's Watson mine needed something nourishing that could also be easily transported and also that would keep while inside the mines, so their loyal wives invented this unique West Virginia specialty. My great-grandfather, Antonio Silletta, was a hand loader there shortly after WWI. This recipe is for him. You are with us always, Poppy.

Whitney Hatcher's Easy Pepperoni Rolls

Boone County native Whitney Rae Hatcher recently moved to Hendersonville, TN, where fresh pepperoni rolls are nowhere to be found. So she creates her own to share with a simple recipe that relies on the classic Pillsbury crescent rolls—perfect if you're pressed for time.

INGREDIENTS:

- 1 container crescent rolls
- 4 sticks of string cheese
- 32 pepperoni slices

Heat oven according to crescent-roll directions. Lay out each crescent, place a few pepperoni slices on each, place a portion of a cheese stick in the center, and roll them up. Bake according to package instructions.

Kaitlynn Anderson's Low-Carb and Gluten-Free Pepperoni Rolls

Kaitlynn Anderson, a native of the Northern Panhandle of West Virginia, moved to Boston in August 2013. Not only did Anderson have difficulty finding pepperoni rolls so far north, it was nearly impossible to find one that fit her low-carb lifestyle.

"It was important for me to find a pepperoni roll recipe that didn't taste like cardboard. One of my favorite recipes is a little higher in calories, but it only has four net carbs," she said. "That brought this delicious taste of home back into my life. Also, since it's gluten-free, my mom and grandmother are able to enjoy pepperoni rolls once again!"

INGREDIENTS:

- 3 tablespoons salted butter
- 4 large eggs
- ½ cup crème fraîche
- ¾ cup full-fat shredded cheese
- 1 cup almond flour
- 3 tablespoons coconut flour
- 4 tablespoons ground psyllium husks
- ½ teaspoon salt
- 2 teaspoons baking powder
- 24 pepperoni slices

Preheat oven to 375 degrees. Kaitlynn uses a convection oven to make sure the heat is evenly distributed. A gas oven may be used, but be sure to pay attention to heat levels and rotate the pan.

Melt 2 tablespoons of butter and set aside. In a medium-to-large mixing bowl, beat eggs with a hand mixer or immersion blender until the eggs are completely blended and look a little frothy. Add melted butter and crème fraîche to the eggs, and mix thoroughly. Mix in ½ cup of the shredded cheese.

In a separate bowl, mix together the remainder of the ingredients except the pepperoni slices. Blend the dry mixture into the egg mixture until a batter forms. Let the mixture rest for 10 minutes.

Line pan with parchment paper. Melt remaining tablespoon of butter and set aside.

Separate the dough into six even portions. Flatten the dough with one hand, and place four of the pepperoni slices in the center. Fold the dough over the slices into a rounded shape. Set on the parchment-paper-covered pan, and repeat with all of the portions.

Drizzle the melted tablespoon of butter over the top of the six rolls, and bake in the oven for 20 to 25 minutes, or until golden brown.

MEMORIES

Kaitlynn Anderson

"Growing up in West Virginia there are things you get used to and miss no matter how far you move away, or how long you're gone. Those things are rolling hills, winding roads, and pepperoni rolls. Those buttery, doughy, meat-filled treats have been a part of my life for as long as I can remember. We sold pepperoni rolls for fundraisers in school, ate them at football games, and spent many sleepovers and movie nights first making pepperoni rolls as our snacks for the rest of the evening."

—Kaitlynn Anderson, a Wellsburg, WV, native

Left: Kaitlynn Anderson's low-carb pepperoni rolls give her a taste of West Virginia while living in Boston. Image Credit: Kaitlynn Anderson.

Momma's Hot Rolls

Amber High, a West Virginia native, moved to the Pacific Northwest with her husband Aaron. They haven't yet met a person out there who has heard of pepperoni rolls, so they've started baking their own as an introduction for their friends. Naturally they run out every time.

"We only use stick pepperoni and jack cheese, and make sure to serve them hot so the inside is extra melty and delicious," Amber said. The dough is made using Aaron's grandma Gussie's recipes for honey rolls, which is modified to include pepperoni in the center before baking. "It's not only extra yummy," Amber said, "but also has a little bit of home baked into every roll."

INGREDIENTS:

- 1¾ cups milk
- 4 tablespoons Crisco
- ½ cup + 1 tablespoon sugar (or honey)
- 2 tablespoons salt
- 2 beaten eggs
- 2 packages dry yeast
- ½ cup warm water
- 7 cups flour (bread flour works best; can use 3 cups whole wheat if desired)
- pepperoni

Heat milk, Crisco, salt, and ½ cup sugar (or honey) until warm and Crisco is melted, and the sugar (honey) and salt are dissolved. Cool to lukewarm.

Mix yeast with warm water, then add 1 teaspoon sugar (or honey). Allow a few minutes to activate (will form "head").

Combine milk mixture, yeast mixture, and eggs. Add 4 cups flour, and beat thoroughly. Add remaining 3 cups flour, and knead lightly. Dough will remain slightly sticky.

Cover with cloth and let rise in warm place for 45 minutes.

Knead dough, cover, and let rise another hour.

Shape into rolls and place on greased pan.

Cover and let rise another 1½ hours. Insert sticks of pepperoni into the center.

Bake at 400 degrees for 15 minutes, until appropriately browned. Remove from oven and brush with butter while hot.

MEMORIES *Cat Pleska*

"You'd think these simple bread rolls were lined in gold, but no, just pepperoni, which in my thinking is really good stuff. I've had pepperoni rolls myself and in truth I did not realize they were developed right in my own state. I never thought about its origins, but certainly I have always enjoyed them. In fact, when a crew of tree cutters from Ohio came by one winter to cut down massive poplars in our yard, we treated them to a lunch of pepperoni rolls and hot coffee. We had no idea they had never heard of pepperoni rolls, just one state over. They were sold on the noshes and bought a half dozen bags of them before they headed home to share with family. How can such a humble and homely little sandwich rate so positively and grandly with most people who try them? It seems like magic, sometimes!"

—Cat Pleska, author of *Riding on Comets: A Memoir* and *One Foot in the Gravy—Hooked on the Sauce: Recipes You'll Relish*

THE FINAL PEPPERONI

No matter how far we roam from home, there is a pepperoni roll-shaped place in our hearts.

The humble, utilitarian pepperoni roll reflects a deep connection to a steadfast, resilient group of people. It's more than the bakeries who produce it or the coal miners who prompted the need or the loyal patrons who have popularized it. It's the understated, hardworking element that translates from food to person, from hand to heart, from snack to soul. It's the culinary embodiment of West Virginia.

Of course, we can all name our favorites. If you're a traditionalist, you're going with Country Club Bakery. If you need it with all the fixings, you're probably a Colasessano's fan. If you want an updated version with cheese and a touch of sweetness, I'd guess Home Industry is your favorite. If you're from Morgantown, it's Chico Bakery. But nothing beats the ones warm from your grandmother's kitchen, because no food is more quintessentially West Virginian.

The pepperoni roll provides a point of pride for West Virginians, people who must often pause to defend our state. We point to our history and legacy—born from the Civil War, born to be hard workers, and born surrounded by the wild and wonderful landscape of the Mountain State. And, we point to the pepperoni roll, universally loved by West Virginians and outsiders alike, saying, yes, great things come from West Virginia, and this is just the tip of the iceberg. Food appeals to everyone, and West Virginians turn out to support our food, our pepperoni roll, to prove that we have created something amazing and to prove that we love pepperoni rolls as much as we love gold and blue, our beautiful mountains, and "Country Roads." Pepperoni rolls are part of who we are.

No matter how far we roam from home, there is a pepperoni roll-shaped place in our hearts. It's the familiar taste beckoning us back to the Mountain State, forever etched into our memories. The pepperoni roll carries with it far more than physical sustenance; it carries lifetimes of memories, experiences, and emotions. The pepperoni roll means a little something different for everyone, but for everyone, it always means West Virginia.

Honorable Michael Aloi   # MEMORIES

To truly enjoy the pepperoni roll, you have to get it fresh and warm.

"First, having a pepperoni roll (we always say we are 'having a pepperoni roll,' not 'eating one'—it shows proper respect for the pepperoni roll) is as much about a memory as the food itself, although how I love eating a pepperoni roll.

"Second, stick pepperoni is the only authentic pepperoni roll, anything else is fraudulent—yes, it is sacrilegious to suggest otherwise.

"One more thing: the pepperoni roll bread is just that, bread, real bread, that has a bite to it, that you have to pull a bit with your teeth. It is not a pastry; the bread should not be soft or sweet. It is simple and you use the same dough that you make your bread with. . . . I fear a future where everyone thinks that a pepperoni roll is sliced pepperoni in a soft, sweet bread. So, you must preserve the truth for posterity.

"One more thing: one should never put American cheese on a pepperoni roll, or pepper jack, it's wrong, all wrong. Mozzarella and provolone are the only acceptable cheeses. God forbid mayonnaise, ketchup, or mustard. Of course, peppers are always appropriate. Colasessano's of Fairmont makes a pepperoni bun (bigger than a roll—it is a bun, not a hoagie or sub). They put sauce (kind of like a hot-dog sauce, spicy, northern West Virginia, not bland), with peppers (Oliverio's) and cheese. I pride myself on being a very tolerant person, embracing that our differences make us better and more interesting, but if God gave me one vote to preserve something authentic, and it is to be left alone, it is the pepperoni roll as originated in Fairmont, WV.

"About memories: I am the grandson of Italian immigrants, and I can't recall when I had my first store-bought pepperoni roll. My early memories are of the pepperoni rolls my grandmother made (Mama Kay Manchin). She would always make them for us when we had band trips or other schools trips on a bus, or when I would go back to college after visiting home or to football games. She would make a lot, two dozen or so, and I would pass them around the bus; they would be gone in less than an hour. People would say, 'What is a pepperoni roll?' and they couldn't understand why we thought it was the greatest food in the world. But then they took a bite, and to see the look on their face—priceless.

"You have to understand some history. The pepperoni roll in central West Virginia had its origins in southern Italy, the region of Calabria. The northern Italians, north of Naples, looked down upon the southern Italians as rural and backwards. So we take pride in the pepperoni roll being 'our food,' kind of like how ramps belong to Appalachia.

"The places where we get our pepperoni rolls are as important as the roll itself. You must get them from a local bakery, anything else is a

Stick pepperoni is the only authentic pepperoni roll, anything else is fraudulent.

People would say, "What is a pepperoni roll?"...

waste of time. I understand if you are starving, but if you want to truly enjoy and savor the pepperoni roll, you must go to the bakery. (Of course, this is only because my grandmother is now deceased, nothing can top that memory. But I must add that my children know how to make a real pepperoni roll, and I love them.) I would always go to Country Club Bakery in Fairmont when I lived and worked there. I knew Cheech Argiro, who claims his father invented the pepperoni roll for commercial purposes, and I accept that Cheech would never lie. Such a good man. He would sit on his stool behind the counter and greet you. The pepperoni roll places only sold pepperoni rolls, and bread and buns, but basically all the same bread. They would sometimes have cookies and drinks in a cooler. It was always so good to see Cheech, and the smell! The smell of bread always brings memories of my childhood and the smell filling the house when my grandmother would bake bread.

"To truly enjoy the pepperoni roll, you have to get it fresh and warm. Today, I went to Tomaro's in Clarksburg (the city that, per capita, simply has the greatest selection of pepperoni rolls in the world—yes, world) and the same women greet me. One went to school with my cousin Timmy; they call me 'honey' or 'Michael,' never 'Judge.' They ask me if I want

But then they took a bite, and to see the look on their face—priceless.

....

some sausage next time they order some. I will usually get half a dozen pepperoni rolls and give some away at the office. The only way to get them is warm, and then they put them in a paper bag. You know they are the real thing when the oils and herbs—the real word is grease—seeps into the paper bag. One of my favorite things to do with a pepperoni roll is to tear it in half and then use it to soak up the olive oil and herbs and tomato juices that remain when you have fresh-sliced tomatoes.

"One more thing and then I will let you go. I remember my grandmother telling me that people would make fun of the Italians when they would bring the homemade bread to school for lunch because it was viewed as perhaps being backward and poor. Proper people brought store-bought bread. So the pepperoni roll reminds me of people I love very much and the struggle they had to endure to make a better life for their children. And so now, today, the food that was looked down upon as that of the poor and unsophisticated, is now the state food, and when I brought it on the school bus, it was special and unique and everyone loved them and wanted one. And yes, that makes me happy."

—Honorable Michael Aloi, US magistrate judge, Clarksburg, WV

REFERENCES

Abruzzino, Chris. Interview with author at Abruzzino's Italian Bakery. April 30, 2015.

Anderson, Colleen. "The Pepperoni Roll." *Goldenseal Magazine*. Spring 2006. http://www.wvculture.org/goldenseal/spring06/pepperoni.html

Anderson, Jimmy. Interview with author at The Donut Shop. May 18, 2015.

Anderson, Kaitlynn. Phone interview with author regarding recipes. December 28, 2015.

Ash, Kelsey. Interview with author regarding Confection Connection. November 24, 2015.

Beckner, Rachelle Bott. "Pepperoni Rolls." *e-WV: The West Virginia Encyclopedia*. June 4, 2013. http://www.wvencyclopedia.org/articles/1837

"The Best of West Virginia Awards." *WV Living*. September 5, 2014. http://www.wvliving.com/Fall-2014/The-Best-of-West-Virginia-Awards/

Bizarre Foods with Andrew Zimmern. "West Virginia Pepperoni Rolls." Travel Channel. February 27, 2012. http://www.travelchannel.com/shows/bizarre-foods/video/west-virginia-pepperoni-rolls

Brown, Joel. Interview with author at Rising Creek Bakery. November 20, 2015.

Brunett, John. Interview with author at Tomaro's Bakery. May 1, 2015.

Brunett, Marisa. Phone interview with author about Tomaro's Bakery. March 30, 2015.

Burnside, Mary Wade. "Pepperoni Rolls." *The Exponent Telegram*. November 15, 2015. http://www.theet.com/lifestyles/featured_stories/pepperoni-rolls/article_d94ec66f-7640-588d-bff5-11cbf0a814e9.html

Daly, Bill. "Calzone v. Stromboli." *Chicago Tribune*. March 26, 2013. http://articles.chicagotribune.com/2013-03-26/features/ct-tribu-daley-question-stromboli-20130326_1_stromboli-calzone-dough

D'Annunzio, Chris. Interview with author at D'Annunzio's Italian Bread. May 3, 2015.

Dean, Josh. "West Virginia's Iconic Pepperoni Roll Is Finally Getting Some Official Recognition." *Bon Appetit*. April 16, 2013. http://www.bonappetit.com/trends/article/west-virginia-s-iconic-pepperoni-roll-is-finally-getting-some-official-recognition

Edge, John. "Fast Food Even Before Fast Food." *New York Times*. September 29, 2009. http://www.nytimes.com/2009/09/30/dining/30unit.html?pagewanted=all&_r=1

Fernandez, Josh. Phone interview with author regarding science of baking. December 29, 2015.

Goalen, Kaitlyn. "The South's Best Cheap Eats Under $10." *Southern Living*. Accessed April 7, 2015. http://www.southernliving.com/travel/souths-best-cheap-meals

Hamrick, Miriah. "The Best of West Virginia Awards 2013." *WV Living*. August 20, 2013.http://www.wvliving.com/Fall-2013/The-Best-of-West-Virginia-Awards/

Harris, Pam and Mike. Interview with author at Home Industry Bakery. April 30, 2015.

Hatcher, Whitney. Phone interview with author regarding recipes. January 1, 2016.

Heffner, Bob. "The Pepperoni Roll Homepage." *Bob Heffner's Pepperoni Roll Page —Fairmont, West Virginia.* August 11, 2002. http://www.bobheffner.com /pepperoniroll/

High, Amber. Phone interview with author regarding recipes. January 5, 2016. http://www.legis.state.wv.us/bill_status/resolution_history .cfm?year=2013&sessiontype=RS&input4=84&billtype=cr&houseorig=h

"House Concurrent Resolution 84." *West Virginia Legislature.* March 19, 2013.

Kayal, Michele. "Pepperoni Rolls: W.Va. with an Italian Accent." *American Food Roots.* March 1, 2013. http://www.americanfoodroots.com/my-american -roots/pepperoni-rolls-west-virginia-with-an-italian-accent/

Kessler, John. "Rise & Dine: The South's Best Breakfast Joints." *Garden & Gun.* August/September 2014. http://gardenandgun.com/article/rise-dine -souths-best-breakfast-joints/page/0/1

"Manchin Congratulates Pepperoni Roll On Being Voted America's Favorite State Food in 'Taste Of America' Contest." *Joe Manchin, United States Senator, West Virginia.* June 14, 2013. http://www.manchin.senate.gov /public/index.cfm/press-releases?ID=c989d831-40ac-45fd-bf65- 5ff8293a400a

Menas, John. Interview with author at Colasessano's World Famous Pizza & Pepperoni Buns. July 2, 2015.

Milam, Bob. Interview with author for American Culinary Federation West Virginia. July 27, 2015.

Miller, Gary. Interview with author at Chico Bakery. June 30, 2015.

Miller, Martha J. "The Pepperoni Rolls of Princeton." *Southern Foodways Alliance.*
        May 27, 2014. http://www.southernfoodways.org/a-helping-of-gravy
        -pepperoni-rolls/

Nelson, Candace. "'Beloved' Pepperoni Roll Wins Contest." *Charleston Daily Mail.*
        June 17, 2013.

———. "Notable West Virginians Nominate Their Favorite State Foods."
        Charleston Daily Mail. April 22, 2013. http://www.wvgazettemail.com/
        article/20130422/DM01/304229991/

———. "Power Park Debuts Colossal Snack." *Charleston Daily Mail.* April 4, 2013.
        http://www.wvgazettemail.com/article/20130422/DM01/304229991/

———. "Resolution Exalts Humble Pepperoni Roll." *Charleston Daily Mail.* March
        20, 2013.

Pallotta, Chris. Interview with author at Country Club Bakery. March 28, 2015.

Parsons, Aaron. Phone interview with author about JR's Donut Castle.
        November 27, 2015.

"The Pepperoni Roll." *Marion County CVB.* Accessed July 18, 2015. http://
        marioncvb.com/pepperoni-roll/

"Pepperoni Rolls." *CooksInfo.com.* Accessed December 19, 2015. http://www
        .cooksinfo.com/pepperoni-rolls

Pogorzelski, John. Interview with author at Monongalia County Ballpark. July 16,
        2015.

Rogers, Steve, Michael Rogers, and Dennis Mazza. Interview with author at
        Rogers and Mazza's Italian Bakery. May 1, 2015.

Roker On The Road. "Regional Secrets." Food Network. http://www.foodnetwork
        .com/shows/roker-on-the-road/2-series/regional-secrets.html.

Stern, Jane and Michael. "Alto Appalachia." *Gourmet Magazine*. January 2007. http://www.gourmet.com/magazine/2000s/2007/01/roadfood-alto -appalachia.html

Timony, Erin. "Iconic Bakery Urges Eating Tomaro's Bread Today." *The State Journal*. July 10, 2014. http://www.statejournal.com/story/25987061/ tomaros-bakery

Todd, Roxy. "Don't Mess with My Pepperoni Roll." *West Virginia Public Broadcasting*. August 18, 2015. http://www.marketplace.org/topics/ business/dont-mess-my-pepperoni-roll

Vingle, Mitch. "Let It Roll: Two Fairmont Institutions Parlay Pepperoni into a Top-Notch Delicacy." *Sunday Gazette Mail*. April 21, 2002.

Ward, Guy. Interview with author regarding West Virginia Three Rivers Festival. May 20, 2015.

Wolfe, Billy. "Sheetz chooses sole pepperoni roll provider." *Charleston Gazette-Mail*. August 17, 2015. http://www.wvgazettemail.com/article/20150817 /GZ01/150819549

———. "W.Va. bakery says losing Sheetz will cost jobs." *Charleston Gazette-Mail*. July 27, 2015. http://www.wvgazettemail.com/article/20150727 /DM06/150729568